ReaLemon
Golden
Anniversary

ReaLemon

Recipe Collection

50 *years of great taste*
50 *years of great recipes with*

ReaLemon

Lemon Juice from Concentrate

1984 marks the 50th Anniversary of ReaLemon® Lemon Juice from Concentrate. To commemorate this special event, we present "The ReaLemon Golden Anniversary Recipe Collection," the best ReaLemon recipes of 50 years.

Since 1934, the ReaLemon brand has stood for quality. Initially, ReaLemon was produced by the Puritan-ReaLemon Company to supply restaurants and hotels. Seven years later, it was offered to consumers in food stores. Then, in 1962, ReaLemon became a member of the Borden family of fine products. Today, we continue in our dedication to bring you ReaLemon products of the unsurpassed quality you have come to expect over the past 50 years.

"The ReaLemon Recipe Collection" features over 200 recipes from appetizers to desserts. Each recipe has been carefully researched, developed and tested by the Borden Kitchens home economists to assure you good taste and convenient preparation.

We are pleased to have you join in the celebration of ReaLemon's Golden Anniversary... 50 Years of Great Taste — 50 Years of Great Recipes! And, we hope you find this collector's edition recipe book a valuable source of new ideas and traditional favorites to delight your family and friends. Good cooking from ReaLemon.

Annie Watts
Annie Watts
Director, Borden Kitchens

Credits

Borden Kitchens:	Annie Watts Cloncs, Director Veda Rose, Senior Home Economist
Design & Production:	Mallard Marketing Associates, Inc. Betsy J. Nagle, Production Mgr. Denny Knittig, Creative Director Donnie Flora, Food Stylist Glenn Peterson, Photographer
Color Separations:	Colorbrite, Inc.
Print Production:	The LeHigh Press, Inc.

Borden, Inc.
180 East Broad Street
Columbus, Ohio 43215

Table of Contents

Appetizers

Tantalizing tidbits to whet the appetite. Choose from this delicious selection of savory spreads, sweet 'n' sour party morsels and refreshing soups for appetizers with the zing of ReaLemon. For easy or elegant entertaining—the right recipe's here.

WARM HERB CHEESE SPREAD

Makes about 4 cups

3 (8-ounce) packages cream cheese, softened
¼ cup milk
¼ cup ReaLemon® Lemon Juice from Concentrate
½ teaspoon *each* basil, oregano, marjoram and thyme leaves
¼ teaspoon garlic powder
½ pound cooked shrimp, chopped (1½ cups), optional

Preheat oven to 350°. In large mixer-bowl, beat cheese just until smooth. Gradually beat in milk then ReaLemon. Stir in remaining ingredients. Pour into 9-inch quiche dish or pie plate. Cover; bake 15 minutes or until hot. Garnish as desired. Serve warm with crackers or fresh vegetables. Refrigerate leftovers.

MICROWAVE: In 9-inch pie plate, prepare cheese spread as above. Microwave on ½ power (medium) 5 to 6 minutes or until hot. Stir before serving.

Pictured: Warm Herb Cheese Spread, Glazed Fruit 'n' Franks (recipe page 6).

GLAZED FRUIT 'N' FRANKS

Makes about 3½ cups

1 cup apricot preserves
⅓ cup ReaLemon® Lemon Juice
    from Concentrate
1 tablespoon cornstarch
½ teaspoon ground cinnamon
1 (8-ounce) package cocktail
    frankfurters *or* ½ pound
    frankfurters, cut into 1-inch
    pieces
1 (8-ounce) can pineapple
    chunks, drained
1 large red apple, cored and cut
    into chunks
1 (11-ounce) can mandarin
    orange segments, drained

In medium saucepan, combine preserves, ReaLemon, cornstarch and cinnamon. Cook and stir until well blended and slightly thickened. Stir in frankfurters and pineapple; heat through. Just before serving, stir in apple and orange. Serve warm. Refrigerate leftovers.

SHRIMP SPREAD

Makes about 3 cups

2 (8-ounce) packages cream
    cheese, softened
¼ cup ReaLemon® Lemon Juice
    from Concentrate
½ pound cooked shrimp,
    chopped (1½ cups)
1 to 2 tablespoons finely
    chopped green onions
1 tablespoon prepared
    horseradish
1 teaspoon Worcestershire sauce
¼ teaspoon pepper
⅛ teaspoon garlic powder

In small mixer bowl, beat cheese until fluffy; gradually beat in ReaLemon. Stir in remaining ingredients. Chill to blend flavors. Garnish as desired. Serve with crackers or fresh vegetables. Refrigerate leftovers.

GAZPACHO

Makes about 1½ quarts

3 firm medium tomatoes, peeled
    (2 quartered, 1 diced)
1 large green pepper
    (½ quartered, ½ diced)
1 large cucumber, pared and
    seeded (½ quartered,
    ½ diced)
1 large onion (½ quartered,
    ½ diced)
2 cloves garlic, finely chopped
3 cups tomato juice
⅓ cup vegetable oil
⅓ cup ReaLemon® Lemon Juice
    from Concentrate
¼ teaspoon hot pepper sauce
2 teaspoons salt
¼ teaspoon pepper
1 cup garlic-flavored croutons
½ cup chopped chives

Place all diced vegetables in individual serving bowls and refrigerate until serving time. In blender container, blend half the quartered vegetables and garlic with ½ *cup* tomato juice until smooth. Repeat with remaining quartered vegetables and ½ *cup* tomato juice. In large bowl, combine pureed mixture, remaining 2 *cups* tomato juice, oil, ReaLemon, hot pepper sauce, salt and pepper; mix well. Chill thoroughly. Serve with diced vegetables, croutons and chives.

WHITE GAZPACHO

Makes about 1½ quarts

4 teaspoons Wyler's® Chicken-Flavor Instant Bouillon *or* 4 Chicken-Flavor Bouillon Cubes

2 cups boiling water

3 medium cucumbers, pared, seeded and cut into cubes (about 3 cups)

1 (16-ounce) container sour cream

2 tablespoons ReaLemon® Lemon Juice from Concentrate

¼ teaspoon garlic powder

¼ teaspoon pepper

In small saucepan, dissolve bouillon in water. Cool completely. In blender or food processor, blend cucumber with ½ *cup* bouillon liquid until smooth. In medium bowl, combine cucumber mixture, remaining bouillon liquid, sour cream, ReaLemon, garlic powder and pepper; mix well. Chill thoroughly. Garnish as desired. Serve with condiments. Refrigerate leftovers.

Suggested Condiments: Chopped fresh tomato, chopped green onions, chopped green pepper, toasted slivered almonds and toasted croutons.

Pictured top to bottom: Sweet 'n' Sour Meatballs, Teriyaki Scallop Roll-Ups, Teriyaki Wing Dings.

SWEET 'N' SOUR MEATBALLS

Makes about 5 dozen

1½ pounds lean ground beef
1 (8-ounce) can water chestnuts, drained and chopped
2 eggs
⅓ cup dry bread crumbs
4 teaspoons Wyler's® Beef-Flavor Instant Bouillon
1 tablespoon Worcestershire sauce
1 cup water
½ cup firmly packed light brown sugar
½ cup ReaLemon® Lemon Juice from Concentrate
¼ cup catsup
2 tablespoons cornstarch
¼ teaspoon salt
1 large red or green pepper, cut into squares
Chopped parsley, optional

In large bowl, combine meat, water chestnuts, eggs, bread crumbs, bouillon and Worcestershire; mix well. Shape into 1¼-inch meatballs. In large skillet, brown meatballs. Remove from pan; pour off fat. In skillet, combine remaining ingredients except pepper and parsley; mix well. Over medium heat, cook and stir until sauce thickens. Reduce heat. Add meatballs; simmer uncovered 10 minutes. Add pepper; heat through. Garnish with parsley if desired. Refrigerate leftovers.

TERIYAKI SCALLOP ROLL-UPS

Makes about 2 dozen

12 slices bacon, partially cooked and cut in half crosswise
⅓ cup ReaLime® Lime Juice from Concentrate
¼ cup soy sauce
¼ cup vegetable oil
1 tablespoon light brown sugar
2 cloves garlic, finely chopped
½ teaspoon pepper
½ pound sea scallops, cut in half
24 fresh pea pods
12 water chestnuts, cut in half

Continued next column

Teriyaki Scallop Roll-Ups

To make teriyaki marinade, combine
ReaLime, soy sauce, oil, sugar, garlic
and pepper; mix well. Wrap 1 scallop
half, 1 pea pod and 1 water chestnut half
in each bacon slice; secure with wooden
pick. Place in shallow baking dish; pour
marinade over. Cover; refrigerate 4
hours or overnight, turning occasionally.
Preheat oven to 450°. Place roll-ups
on rack in aluminum foil-lined shallow
baking pan; bake 6 minutes. Turn;
continue baking 6 minutes or until
bacon is crisp. Serve hot. Refrigerate
leftovers.

TERIYAKI WING DINGS

Makes about 3 dozen

**⅓ cup ReaLemon® Lemon Juice
  from Concentrate**
¼ cup catsup
¼ cup soy sauce
¼ cup vegetable oil
2 tablespoons brown sugar
¼ teaspoon garlic powder
¼ teaspoon pepper
**3 pounds chicken wing drumettes
  or chicken wings, cut at joints
  and wing tips removed**

To make teriyaki marinade, combine all
ingredients except chicken; mix well.
Place chicken in shallow baking dish;
pour marinade over. Cover; refrigerate
overnight, turning occasionally. Preheat
oven to 375°. Arrange chicken on rack
in aluminum foil-lined shallow baking
pan. Bake 40 to 45 minutes, basting
occasionally with marinade. Refrigerate
leftovers.

MICROWAVE: Prepare chicken as
above. Divide chicken and marinade
between two 8-inch square baking
dishes. Cover with wax paper; microwave each dish on full power (high) 12 to
14 minutes or until tender, rearranging
pieces once or twice.

RUMAKI

Makes 2 dozen

**¼ cup ReaLemon® Lemon Juice
  from Concentrate**
¼ cup soy sauce
¼ cup vegetable oil
3 tablespoons catsup
2 cloves garlic, finely chopped
½ teaspoon pepper
**12 chicken livers, cut in half
  (about ½ pound)**
8 water chestnuts, cut in thirds
**12 slices bacon, cut in half
  crosswise**
Brown sugar

To make marinade, combine ReaLemon,
soy sauce, oil, catsup, garlic and pepper; mix well. Wrap 1 liver half and 1
water chestnut slice in each bacon slice;
secure with wooden pick. Place in shallow baking dish; pour marinade over.
Cover; refrigerate 4 hours or overnight,
turning occasionally. Preheat oven to
450°. Roll Rumaki in brown sugar; place
on rack in aluminum foil-lined shallow
baking pan. Bake 10 minutes. Turn;
continue baking 15 minutes or until
bacon is crisp. Serve hot. Refrigerate
leftovers.

Rumaki

SHRIMP AND MUSHROOMS

Makes about 3 dozen

⅓ cup margarine or butter
⅓ cup dry vermouth or dry white wine
¼ cup ReaLemon® Lemon Juice from Concentrate
3 cloves garlic, finely chopped
½ teaspoon salt
¼ teaspoon pepper
8 ounces small whole fresh mushrooms (about 2 cups)
1 pound medium raw shrimp, peeled and deveined (about 36)
Chopped parsley

In large skillet or chafing dish, melt margarine; add remaining ingredients except shrimp and parsley. Over medium heat, cook 5 to 8 minutes. Add shrimp; cook until tender, about 3 minutes. Garnish with parsley. Serve hot. Refrigerate leftovers.

MICROWAVE: In 12x7-inch baking dish, microwave margarine on full power (high) 1 minute or until melted. Add remaining ingredients except shrimp; microwave on full power (high) 3 to 4 minutes. Add shrimp; microwave on full power (high) 4 to 5 minutes or until shrimp is tender. Serve as above.

MARINATED VEGETABLES ▲

Makes 4 cups

4 cups assorted fresh vegetables*
¼ cup ReaLemon® Lemon Juice from Concentrate
¼ cup vegetable oil
1 tablespoon sugar
1 teaspoon salt
½ teaspoon oregano or thyme leaves
⅛ teaspoon pepper

Place vegetables in 1½-quart shallow baking dish. In small bowl or jar, combine remaining ingredients; mix well. Pour over vegetables. Cover; refrigerate 6 hours or overnight, stirring occasionally. Serve as appetizer or on lettuce leaves as salad.

***Suggested Vegetables:** Cauliflowerets, carrots, mushrooms, cherry tomatoes, brussel sprouts, broccoli flowerets, zucchini, onion or cucumber.

Tip: Recipe can be doubled.

GREEK LEMON SOUP

Makes about 1 quart

4 teaspoons Wyler's® Chicken-Flavor Instant Bouillon or 4 Chicken-Flavor Bouillon Cubes
4 cups boiling water
⅓ cup uncooked long grain rice
3 eggs
¼ cup ReaLemon® Lemon Juice from Concentrate

In large saucepan, dissolve bouillon in water; add rice. Cover and simmer 25 minutes. In small bowl, beat eggs and ReaLemon. Gradually stir about ½ cup hot bouillon mixture into eggs; stir into hot soup. Serve immediately. Refrigerate leftovers.

SCANDINAVIAN RASPBERRY SOUP

Makes 8 to 10 servings

2 (10-ounce) packages frozen
  red raspberries in syrup,
  thawed
½ cup orange juice
¼ cup ReaLemon® Lemon Juice
  from Concentrate
1 tablespoon cornstarch
¾ cup chablis or other dry
  white wine
Fresh orange sections
Raspberries, orange rind twists
  or mint leaves for garnish
Sour cream

In blender container, puree *1 package*
raspberries; strain to remove seeds. In
medium saucepan, combine pureed
raspberries, orange juice, ReaLemon
and cornstarch; mix well. Over medium
heat, cook and stir until slightly thickened
and clear; cool. Stir in remaining package raspberries and chablis. Chill. To
serve, place several orange sections in
each bowl; add soup. Garnish as
desired; serve with sour cream.
Refrigerate leftovers.

Scandinavian Raspberry Soup

GUACAMOLE

Makes about 1½ cups

2 ripe medium avocados, seeded
  and peeled
2 tablespoons ReaLime® Lime
  Juice from Concentrate *or*
  ReaLemon® Lemon Juice
  from Concentrate
1 tablespoon finely chopped
  onion
1 teaspoon seasoned salt
¼ teaspoon hot pepper sauce
¼ teaspoon garlic powder

In medium bowl or blender, mash
avocados. Add remaining ingredients;
mix well. Chill thoroughly to blend
flavors. Garnish as desired. Serve with
tortilla chips. Refrigerate leftovers.

Variations: Add 1 or more of the follow-
ing: sour cream, crumbled bacon,
coarsely chopped water chestnuts,
chopped tomato, chopped chilies.

Salads

No matter what the meal—pick the perfect salad from this garden medley of recipes. ReaLemon® Lemon Juice from Concentrate adds fresh light flavor to hearty main dish salads of chicken or shrimp, crisp vegetable creations and quick homemade dressings.

MARINATED CONFETTI COLESLAW

Makes 6 to 8 servings

5 cups coarsely shredded cabbage (about 1 pound)
1 firm large tomato, seeded and diced
½ cup chopped green pepper
⅓ cup sliced green onions
½ cup ReaLemon® Lemon Juice from Concentrate
⅓ cup sugar
⅓ cup vegetable oil
1 teaspoon salt
½ teaspoon dry mustard

In medium bowl, combine cabbage, tomato, pepper and onions. In small saucepan, combine remaining ingredients; bring to a boil. Pour over vegetables. Cover; chill 4 hours or overnight to blend flavors.

Pictured: Marinated Confetti Coleslaw; Tropical Chicken Salad and Sweet Onion Dressing (recipes page 14).

13

TROPICAL CHICKEN SALAD

Makes 4 to 6 servings

- 4 cups cubed cooked chicken or turkey
- 2 large oranges, peeled, sectioned and drained
- 1½ cups cut-up fresh pineapple, drained
- 1 cup seedless green grape halves
- 1 cup sliced celery
- ¾ cup mayonnaise or salad dressing
- 3 to 4 tablespoons ReaLemon® Lemon Juice from Concentrate
- ½ teaspoon ground ginger
- ½ teaspoon salt
- ½ to ¾ cup cashews

In large bowl, combine chicken, fruit and celery; chill. In small bowl, combine remaining ingredients except nuts; chill. Just before serving, combine chicken mixture, dressing and nuts. Serve in hollowed out pineapple shells or on lettuce leaves. Refrigerate leftovers.

SWEET ONION DRESSING

Makes about 2 cups

- 1 cup vegetable oil
- ⅔ cup sugar
- ⅓ cup ReaLemon® Lemon Juice from Concentrate
- ⅓ cup catsup
- 1 small onion, cut up
- 1 tablespoon Worcestershire sauce

In blender or food processor, combine ingredients; blend until smooth. Chill to blend flavors.

Hand Mix Method: Grate onion. In 1-pint jar with tight-fitting lid or cruet, combine ingredients; shake well. (Dressing will be slightly thinner.)

LINGUINE TUNA SALAD

Makes 6 servings

- 1 (7-ounce) package Creamette® Linguine, broken in half
- ¼ cup ReaLemon® Lemon Juice from Concentrate
- ¼ cup vegetable oil
- ¼ cup chopped green onions
- 2 teaspoons sugar
- 1 teaspoon Italian seasoning
- 1 teaspoon seasoned salt
- 1 (12½-ounce) can tuna, drained
- 1 (10-ounce) package frozen green peas, thawed
- 2 firm medium tomatoes, chopped

Cook linguine according to package directions; drain. Meanwhile, in large bowl, combine ReaLemon, oil, onions, sugar, Italian seasoning and salt; mix well. Add *hot* linguine; toss. Add remaining ingredients; mix well. Cover; chill to blend flavors. Serve on lettuce; garnish as desired. Refrigerate leftovers.

Linguine Tuna Salad

GAZPACHO GARDEN SALAD ▶

Makes 8 servings

- ½ cup vegetable oil
- ⅓ cup ReaLemon® Lemon Juice from Concentrate
- 2 cloves garlic, finely chopped
- 1½ teaspoons salt
- ¼ teaspoon pepper
- 1 medium green pepper, seeded and diced
- 2 firm medium tomatoes, diced
- 1 medium cucumber, pared, seeded and diced
- ½ cup sliced green onions

In 1-pint jar with tight-fitting lid or cruet, combine oil, ReaLemon, garlic, salt and pepper; shake well. In narrow 1-quart glass container, layer half each of the green pepper, tomatoes, cucumber and onions; repeat layering with remaining vegetables. Pour dressing over salad. Cover; chill 4 hours to blend flavors.

WILTED LETTUCE

Makes 6 servings

- ½ pound bacon, cooked and crumbled, reserving ¼ cup drippings
- ½ cup finely chopped onion
- ⅓ cup ReaLemon® Lemon Juice from Concentrate
- ⅓ cup water
- 3 tablespoons sugar
- ½ pound leaf lettuce, torn into bite-size pieces (about 8 cups)

In large skillet, cook onion in drippings until tender. Stir in ReaLemon, water and sugar; heat through. Pour over lettuce; toss until wilted. Garnish with bacon. Refrigerate leftovers.

MICROWAVE: Microwave bacon, reserving ¼ *cup* drippings. In 12x7-inch baking dish, combine reserved drippings and onion; cover with wax paper. Microwave on full power (high) 3 minutes. Add ReaLemon, water and sugar; microwave on full power (high) 3 to 4 minutes. Proceed as above.

MINTED MELON MOLD ▲

Makes 8 to 10 servings

1½ cups boiling water
1 (3-ounce) package lemon
   flavor gelatin
1 (3-ounce) package lime flavor
   gelatin
¾ cup ReaLime® Lime Juice from
   Concentrate
½ cup cold water
⅛ teaspoon peppermint extract
2 cups melon balls (cantaloupe,
   honeydew, etc.)
   Lettuce leaves
   Coconut Cream Dressing
   Mint leaves and additional
   melon balls, optional

In medium bowl, pour boiling water
over gelatins; stir until dissolved. Add
ReaLime, cold water and extract; chill
until partially set. Fold in melon. Pour
into lightly oiled 5-cup ring mold. Chill
until set, about 3 hours or overnight.
Unmold onto lettuce. Serve with
Coconut Cream Dressing; garnish with
mint and melon balls if desired.

Continued next column

Coconut Cream Dressing

½ cup sour cream
3 tablespoons flaked coconut
1 tablespoon honey
1 tablespoon ReaLime® Lime
   Juice from Concentrate

In small bowl, combine all ingredients;
mix well. Chill before serving. Refrigerate leftovers. (Makes about ½ cup)

CELERY SEED DRESSING

Makes about 1 cup

½ cup sugar
¼ cup ReaLemon® Lemon Juice
   from Concentrate
2 teaspoons cider vinegar
1 teaspoon dry mustard
½ teaspoon salt
½ cup vegetable oil
1 teaspoon celery seed or poppy
   seed

In blender container, combine all
ingredients except oil and celery seed;
blend until smooth. On low speed,
continue blending, slowly adding oil.
Stir in celery seed. Chill to blend
flavors.

CHERRY WALDORF GELATIN ▲

Makes 8 to 10 servings

2 cups boiling water
1 (6-ounce) package cherry
   flavor gelatin
1 cup cold water
¼ cup ReaLemon® Lemon Juice
   from Concentrate
1½ cups chopped apples
1 cup chopped celery
½ cup chopped walnuts or
   pecans
Lettuce leaves
Apple slices and celery leaves,
   optional

In medium bowl, pour boiling water
over gelatin; stir until dissolved. Add
cold water and ReaLemon; chill until
partially set. Fold in apples, celery and
nuts. Pour into lightly oiled 6-cup mold
or 9-inch square baking pan. Chill until
set, 4 to 6 hours or overnight. Serve on
lettuce. Garnish with apple and celery
leaves if desired.

PERFECTION SALAD

Makes 8 to 10 servings

2 envelopes unflavored gelatine
⅓ cup ReaLemon® Lemon Juice
   from Concentrate
2¾ cups water
½ cup sugar
¼ cup cider vinegar
½ teaspoon salt
2 cups finely shredded cabbage
1 cup chopped celery
½ cup chopped green pepper
1 (2-ounce) jar pimientos,
   drained and chopped

In medium saucepan, soften gelatine in
ReaLemon; let stand 1 minute. Over
low heat, cook until gelatine dissolves.
Add water, sugar, vinegar and salt; stir
until sugar dissolves. Chill until partially
set. Fold in remaining ingredients; pour
into lightly oiled 6-cup mold. Chill until
set, about 3 hours or overnight. Refrigerate leftovers.

GARDEN MEDLEY BEAN SALAD

Makes 8 to 10 servings

1 (9-ounce) package frozen cut green beans, cooked and drained
1 (10-ounce) package frozen green lima beans, cooked and drained
⅔ cup ReaLemon® Lemon Juice from Concentrate
⅓ cup sugar
⅓ cup vegetable oil
1 teaspoon salt
½ teaspoon basil leaves
⅛ teaspoon pepper
8 ounces fresh mushrooms, cut in half (about 2 cups)
1 pint cherry tomatoes, cut in half

In 1-pint jar with tight-fitting lid, combine ReaLemon, sugar, oil, salt, basil and pepper; shake well. In 1½-quart shallow baking dish, combine green beans, lima beans and mushrooms. Pour dressing over vegetables. Cover; refrigerate 3 hours or overnight, stirring occasionally. Before serving, add tomatoes.

ITALIAN VEGETABLE SALAD

Makes 10 to 12 servings

1 cup vegetable oil
⅔ cup ReaLemon® Lemon Juice from Concentrate
½ cup water
¼ cup sugar
2 teaspoons salt
1 teaspoon oregano leaves
½ teaspoon pepper
1 small head cauliflower, separated into flowerets
4 medium carrots, pared and cut into 2-inch strips
4 ribs celery, cut into 1-inch pieces
1 (4- to 6-ounce) jar pimiento-stuffed olives

In large saucepan, combine oil, ReaLemon, water, sugar, salt, oregano and pepper; bring to a boil. Add remaining ingredients except olives; cover and simmer 5 minutes. Add olives; pour into medium bowl. Cover; chill overnight to blend flavors. Drain before serving.

HONEYED ORANGE DRESSING

Makes about 1¼ cups

½ cup vegetable oil
⅓ cup orange juice
¼ cup ReaLime® Lime Juice from Concentrate
3 tablespoons honey
1 teaspoon garlic salt
¼ teaspoon celery seed

In 1-pint jar with tight-fitting lid or cruet, combine ingredients; shake well. Chill to blend flavors.

BACON & EGG POTATO SALAD

Makes 10 to 12 servings

**5 cups cooked, peeled and
 cubed potatoes (about 2
 pounds)**
¼ cup chopped green onions
**⅓ cup ReaLemon® Lemon Juice
 from Concentrate**
⅓ cup water
¼ cup vegetable oil
1½ teaspoons celery salt
**1 teaspoon Worcestershire
 sauce**
½ teaspoon dry mustard
¼ teaspoon pepper
**4 slices bacon, cooked and
 crumbled**
3 hard-cooked eggs, chopped
¼ cup grated Parmesan cheese
3 tablespoons chopped parsley

In large bowl, combine potatoes and
onions. In small saucepan, combine
ReaLemon, water, oil, celery salt,
Worcestershire, mustard and pepper;
bring to a boil. Pour over potato mixture; mix well. Cover; chill overnight to
blend flavors. Remove from refrigerator
30 minutes before serving; stir in
bacon, eggs, Parmesan cheese and
parsley. Refrigerate leftovers.

Bacon & Egg Potato Salad

LEMON MAYONNAISE

Makes about 1 cup

¾ cup vegetable oil
**2 tablespoons ReaLemon® Lemon
 Juice from Concentrate**
1 egg*
½ teaspoon salt
½ teaspoon dry mustard

In blender container, combine ¼ cup
oil and remaining ingredients; blend
until smooth. On low speed, continue
blending; slowly add remaining ½ cup
oil. Chill to blend flavors. Store in
refrigerator.

Fruit Dressing: Add 1 cup thawed
frozen non-dairy whipped topping and
2 tablespoons thawed frozen orange
juice concentrate to 1 cup mayonnaise;
mix well. Refrigerate. (Makes 2 cups)

Thousand Island: Add ½ cup chili
sauce, 1 chopped hard-cooked egg, ¼
cup *each* finely chopped onion, green
pepper and drained pickle relish to 1
cup mayonnaise; mix well. Refrigerate.
(Makes about 2 cups)

Horseradish Sauce: Add 2 teaspoons
prepared horseradish to ½ *cup* mayonnaise. Refrigerate. (Makes ½ cup)

*Use only Grade A clean, uncracked
 egg.

DILL SEAFOOD SALAD

Makes 12 servings

1½ pounds small raw shrimp,
   peeled, deveined and cooked
1½ pounds sea scallops, cooked
   and chopped or bay scallops,
   cooked
½ cup chopped celery
¼ cup finely chopped onion
1 tablespoon prepared mustard
1 cup mayonnaise or salad
   dressing
¼ cup ReaLemon® Lemon Juice
   from Concentrate
1 teaspoon dill weed
¾ teaspoon salt
¼ teaspoon pepper

In large bowl, combine ingredients; mix
well. Cover; chill to blend flavors.
Refrigerate leftovers.

HOT CHICKEN SALAD

Makes 4 to 6 servings

2 cups cubed cooked chicken or
   turkey
1 cup chopped celery
1 (8-ounce) can water chestnuts,
   drained and coarsely
   chopped
2 tablespoons finely chopped
   onion
1 cup mayonnaise or salad
   dressing
3 tablespoons ReaLemon®
   Lemon Juice from
   Concentrate
1 teaspoon Wyler's® Chicken-
   Flavor Instant Bouillon
2 tablespoons sliced almonds,
   toasted
2 tablespoons chopped parsley

Preheat oven to 350°. In large bowl,
combine all ingredients except almonds
and parsley. Turn into 1½-quart baking
dish; top with almonds. Bake 20 minutes
or until hot. Garnish with parsley.
Refrigerate leftovers.

Continued next column

Hot Chicken Salad

MICROWAVE: Prepare salad as above
in 1½-quart baking dish. Microwave on
full power (high) 5 to 6 minutes or until
hot. Stir before serving. Garnish with
parsley.

MARINATED ORIENTAL BEEF SALAD

Makes 4 servings

1 (1- to 1¼-pound) flank steak
⅓ cup ReaLemon® Lemon Juice
   from Concentrate
¼ cup catsup
¼ cup vegetable oil
1 tablespoon brown sugar
¼ teaspoon garlic powder
¼ teaspoon ground ginger
¼ teaspoon pepper
8 ounces fresh mushrooms,
   sliced (about 2 cups)
1 (8-ounce) can sliced water
   chestnuts, drained
1 medium sweet onion, sliced
   and separated into rings
1 (6-ounce) package frozen pea
   pods, thawed, or 4 ounces
   fresh pea pods
Lettuce leaves
Tomato wedges

Broil meat 5 minutes on each side or
until desired doneness; slice diagonally
into thin strips. Meanwhile, in large
bowl, combine ReaLemon, catsup, oil,
sugar, garlic powder, ginger and
pepper; mix well. Add mushrooms,
water chestnuts and onion; mix well.
Cover; refrigerate 8 hours or overnight,
stirring occasionally. Before serving,
add pea pods. Serve on lettuce; garnish
with tomato. Refrigerate leftovers.

MEDITERRANEAN TUNA SALAD

Makes 4 servings

2 (10-ounce) packages frozen
    chopped broccoli, thawed
    and well drained
1 (10-ounce) can tuna, drained
    and flaked
1 firm large tomato, cubed
¼ cup sliced pitted ripe olives
1 (0.7-ounce) package Italian
    salad dressing mix
½ cup vegetable oil
⅓ cup ReaLemon® Lemon Juice
    from Concentrate
2 tablespoons water
⅛ teaspoon garlic powder

In large bowl, combine broccoli, tuna,
tomato and olives. In 1-pint jar with
tight-fitting lid or cruet, combine salad
dressing mix, oil, ReaLemon, water and
garlic powder; shake well. Pour over
tuna mixture; mix well. Cover; chill to
blend flavors. Refrigerate leftovers.

DILLY CUCUMBER SALAD ▲

Makes 4 servings

1 (8-ounce) container sour cream
¼ cup ReaLemon® Lemon Juice
    from Concentrate
3 tablespoons sugar
1 teaspoon salt
½ teaspoon dill weed
1 medium cucumber, sliced
1 medium sweet white onion,
    sliced and separated into
    rings

In medium bowl, combine sour cream,
ReaLemon, sugar, salt and dill weed;
mix well. Add cucumber and onion.
Cover; chill to blend flavors.

Tip: Recipe can be doubled.

VERSATILE LEMON DRESSING

Makes about 1⅓ cups

½ cup ReaLemon® Lemon Juice
    from Concentrate
½ cup vegetable oil
⅓ cup white *or* red wine
2 tablespoons grated Parmesan
    cheese
2 teaspoons sugar
¾ teaspoon garlic salt
½ teaspoon pepper
½ teaspoon thyme leaves

In 1-pint jar with tight-fitting lid or cruet,
combine ingredients; shake well. Chill
to blend flavors. Use as salad dressing
or marinade.

To Use As Marinade: In shallow baking
dish, pour dressing over chicken parts,
salmon, haddock or other firm-fleshed
fish; marinate several hours or overnight. Bake, grill or broil to desired
doneness.

TABBOULEH SALAD

Makes 6 servings

1 tablespoon Wyler's® Chicken-
    Flavor Instant Bouillon
7 cups boiling water
1¾ cups bulgur wheat
1 large firm tomato, chopped
1 small zucchini, chopped
¼ cup sliced pitted ripe olives
¼ cup sliced green onions
¼ cup ReaLemon® Lemon Juice
    from Concentrate
¼ cup vegetable or olive oil
1 tablespoon chopped parsley
½ teaspoon basil *or* 1 teaspoon
    dried mint leaves
½ teaspoon garlic salt

Dissolve bouillon in water; add bulgur.
Let stand 2 to 3 hours; drain thoroughly.
Turn into large bowl; chill. Add remaining ingredients; mix well. Cover; chill to
blend flavors.

Variation: To make a rice salad, omit
bulgur and water. Cook 1 cup long grain
rice according to label directions, using
1 tablespoon Wyler's® Chicken-Flavor
Instant Bouillon instead of salt. Proceed as above.

LEMONY LOW CAL DRESSING

Makes about 1 cup; 8 calories per
tablespoon

¼ cup ReaLemon® Lemon Juice
    from Concentrate
⅔ cup plus 2 tablespoons water
1 (1.3-ounce) package low
    calorie Italian salad dressing
    mix

In 1-pint jar with tight-fitting lid or cruet,
combine ingredients; shake well. Chill
to blend flavors.

CHICKEN SALAD SUPREME ▲

Makes 4 to 6 servings

1 cup mayonnaise or salad
    dressing
¼ cup ReaLime® Lime Juice from
    Concentrate
1 teaspoon salt
¼ teaspoon ground nutmeg
4 cups cubed cooked chicken or
    turkey
1 (11-ounce) can mandarin
    orange segments, drained
1 cup seedless green grape
    halves
¾ cup chopped celery
½ cup slivered almonds, toasted

In large bowl, combine mayonnaise,
ReaLime, salt and nutmeg. Add remaining ingredients; mix well. Chill. Serve
on lettuce. Refrigerate leftovers.

LIME FRENCH DRESSING

Makes about ⅔ cup

½ cup vegetable oil
3 tablespoons ReaLime® Lime
   Juice from Concentrate *or*
   ReaLemon® Lemon Juice
   from Concentrate
2 teaspoons sugar
1 teaspoon garlic powder
1 teaspoon dry mustard
½ teaspoon salt
¼ teaspoon pepper

In small jar with tight-fitting lid or cruet,
combine ingredients; shake well. Chill
to blend flavors.

Lime French Dressing shown with salad of
greens, cauliflowerets, bacon and Parmesan
cheese.

ORIENTAL SHRIMP SALAD WITH PUFF BOWL ▶

Makes 6 servings

¾ cup mayonnaise or salad
   dressing
¼ cup ReaLemon® Lemon Juice
   from Concentrate
1 tablespoon prepared
   horseradish
¼ to ½ teaspoon garlic salt
1 pound small raw shrimp,
   peeled, deveined and cooked
1 (6-ounce) package frozen pea
   pods, thawed, or 4 ounces
   fresh pea pods
1 (8-ounce) can sliced water
   chestnuts, drained
1 cup sliced fresh mushrooms
   (about 4 ounces)
1 cup diagonally sliced celery
2 ounces fresh bean sprouts
   (about 1 cup)
¼ cup sliced green onions
   Puff Bowl, optional

In large bowl, combine mayonnaise,
ReaLemon, horseradish and garlic salt.
Add remaining ingredients except Puff
Bowl; mix well. Cover; chill to blend
flavors. Just before serving, spoon into
Puff Bowl or lettuce leaves. Refrigerate
leftovers.

Puff Bowl

2 eggs
½ cup unsifted flour
½ cup milk
¼ teaspoon salt
2 tablespoons margarine or
   butter, melted

Preheat oven to 425°. In small mixer
bowl, beat eggs until frothy. Gradually
beat in flour; beat until smooth. Add
milk, salt and margarine; mix well. Pour
into well-greased 9-inch pie plate. Bake
15 minutes. Reduce oven temperature
to 350°; continue baking 10 to 15
minutes or until browned. Cool.

DIETER'S MOCK MAYONNAISE

Makes about 1 cup; 20 calories per
tablespoon

1 cup lowfat cottage cheese
2 tablespoons ReaLemon®
Lemon Juice from
Concentrate
2 egg yolks
Dash cayenne pepper
¼ teaspoon prepared mustard
¼ teaspoon onion powder

In blender container, blend cottage
cheese until smooth. Add ReaLemon,
egg yolks, pepper, mustard and onion
powder; blend until smooth. Chill to
blend flavors. Store in refrigerator.

LEMON SPICED FRUIT

Makes 6 to 8 servings

1 (29-ounce) can peach or
apricot halves, drained,
reserving syrup
½ cup sugar
¼ cup ReaLemon® Lemon Juice
from Concentrate
12 whole cloves
1 cinnamon stick

In medium saucepan, combine reserved syrup, sugar, ReaLemon, cloves
and cinnamon; bring to a boil. Reduce
heat; add fruit. Simmer uncovered
10 minutes. Chill 4 hours or overnight
to blend flavors. Serve as salad or meat
accompaniment.

MICROWAVE: In 1½- to 2-quart round
baking dish, combine reserved syrup,
sugar, ReaLemon, cloves and cinnamon. Microwave on full power (high)
4½ to 5 minutes or until mixture boils.
Add fruit; microwave at ⅓ power (low)
5 minutes. Proceed as above.

Beverages

From a variety of lemonades to spectacular party punches and warm winter toddies, here's a bevy of beverages for every occasion. Serve Southern Sunshine to brighten your next brunch or Strawberry Watermelon Slush for a refreshing summer cooler.

LEMONADE

Sugar
ReaLemon® Lemon Juice from
Concentrate
Cold Water

Dissolve sugar in ReaLemon; add cold water. Serve over ice. Garnish as desired.

To Make:

1 serving (8 ounces)	2 tablespoons sugar 2 tablespoons ReaLemon ¾ cup cold water
1 quart	½ cup sugar ½ cup ReaLemon 3¼ cups cold water
1 gallon	2 cups sugar 2 cups ReaLemon 3 quarts plus 1 cup cold water
2 gallons	4 cups sugar 1 (32-ounce) bottle ReaLemon 6½ quarts cold water

Minted Lemonade: Stir in 2 or 3 drops peppermint extract to 1 quart lemonade.

Pink Lemonade: Stir in 1 to 2 teaspoons grenadine syrup *or* 1 or 2 drops red food coloring to 1 quart lemonade.

Slushy Lemonade: In blender container, combine ½ cup ReaLemon and ½ cup sugar with 1 cup water; add ice to make 1 quart. Blend until smooth. Serve immediately. Makes about 1 quart.

Sparkling Lemonade: Substitute club soda for cold water.

27

HOT SPICED LEMONADE

Makes about 4 cups

3 cups water
⅔ cup firmly packed light brown sugar
½ cup ReaLemon® Lemon Juice from Concentrate
8 whole cloves
2 cinnamon sticks
Additional cinnamon sticks for garnish, optional

In medium saucepan, combine all ingredients except garnish. Simmer uncovered 20 minutes to blend flavors; remove spices. Serve hot in mugs with cinnamon sticks if desired.

MICROWAVE: In 1-quart glass measure, combine ingredients as above. Microwave on full power (high) 4 to 5 minutes or until heated through. Serve as above.

CLARET LEMONADE

Makes about 6 cups

3¼ cups cold water
½ cup ReaLemon® Lemon Juice from Concentrate
½ cup sugar
2 cups claret wine, chilled
Ice

In pitcher, combine water, ReaLemon and sugar; stir until sugar dissolves. Just before serving, stir in wine; serve over ice.

LEMONADE SYRUP BASE

Makes about 3⅔ cups

2 cups sugar
½ cup water
2 cups ReaLemon® Lemon Juice from Concentrate

In medium saucepan, combine sugar and water. Over low heat, cook until sugar dissolves, stirring occasionally; add ReaLemon. Cool. Store covered in refrigerator.

For 1 (8-ounce) serving: Pour ⅓ cup lemonade syrup into glass; add ⅔ cup cold water. Stir; add ice.

For 1 quart: In pitcher, combine 1⅓ cups lemonade syrup and 2⅔ cups cold water; stir. Add ice.

◀ STRAWBERRY LEMONADE

Makes about 2 quarts

1 quart fresh strawberries, cleaned and hulled
3 cups cold water
¾ cup ReaLemon® Lemon Juice from Concentrate
¾ to 1 cup sugar
2 cups club soda, chilled
Ice
Strawberries and mint leaves for garnish, optional

In blender container, blend strawberries well. In pitcher, combine pureed strawberries, water, ReaLemon and sugar; stir until sugar dissolves. Add club soda. Serve over ice; garnish with strawberries and mint if desired.

WHITE SANGRIA ▶

Makes about 2 quarts

½ to ¾ cup sugar
½ cup ReaLemon® Lemon Juice
   from Concentrate, chilled
¼ cup ReaLime® Lime Juice from
   Concentrate, chilled
1 (750 mL) bottle sauterne, chilled
¼ cup orange-flavored liqueur
1 (32-ounce) bottle club soda,
   chilled
   Orange, plum or nectarine
   slices, green grapes or other
   fresh fruit
   Ice

In pitcher, combine sugar, ReaLemon
and ReaLime; stir until sugar dissolves.
Add sauterne and orange-flavored
liqueur. Just before serving, add club
soda, fruit and ice.

RED SANGRIA

Makes about 2 quarts

¾ cup sugar
¾ cup orange juice, chilled
⅓ cup ReaLemon® Lemon Juice
   from Concentrate
⅓ cup ReaLime® Lime Juice from
   Concentrate
6 cups medium-dry red wine,
   chilled
   Orange, peach or plum slices or
   grapes
   Ice

In pitcher, combine sugar, orange juice,
ReaLemon and ReaLime; stir until
sugar dissolves. Just before serving,
add wine, fruit and ice.

WHITE SANGRITA

Makes about 7 cups

3 cups catawba or other white
   grape juice
½ cup ReaLemon® Lemon Juice
   from Concentrate
½ cup sugar
1 (32-ounce) bottle club soda,
   chilled
   Green grapes, strawberries and
   orange slices
   Ice

In pitcher, combine grape juice,
ReaLemon and sugar; stir until sugar
dissolves. Just before serving, add club
soda and fruit. Serve over ice.

CRANBERRY ORANGE PUNCH ▲

Makes about 3½ quarts

2 (32-ounce) bottles cranberry
  juice cocktail, chilled
1½ cups ReaLemon® Lemon Juice
  from Concentrate
⅔ cup sugar
2 (16-ounce) bottles orange soda,
  chilled
½ cup orange-flavored liqueur,
  optional
  Ice block or ice ring
1 orange, sliced
  Whole cloves and cranberries,
  optional

In large punch bowl, combine cranberry juice, ReaLemon and sugar; stir
until sugar dissolves. Just before
serving, add orange soda and liqueur if
desired; add ice. Garnish with orange
slices decorated with cloves and
cranberries if desired.

HOT CRANBERRY PUNCH

Makes about 1½ quarts

1 (32-ounce) bottle cranberry
  juice cocktail
2 cups orange juice
¾ cup firmly packed light brown
  sugar
½ cup ReaLemon® Lemon Juice
  from Concentrate
3 whole cloves
2 cinnamon sticks

In large saucepan, combine ingredients; bring to a boil. Reduce heat;
simmer uncovered 10 minutes. Remove
spices. Serve warm.

SPIRITED CRANBERRY PUNCH

Makes about 3 quarts

Cranberry Ice Star Mold, optional
6 cups cranberry juice cocktail, chilled
1½ cups pineapple juice, chilled
¾ cup ReaLemon® Lemon Juice from Concentrate
1 (32-ounce) bottle ginger ale, chilled
1 cup cranberry-flavored liqueur

Prepare ice mold in advance. In punch bowl, combine cranberry juice, pineapple juice and ReaLemon. Just before serving, add ginger ale and liqueur; add Cranberry Ice Star Mold if desired.

Cranberry Ice Star Mold

2 cups cranberry juice cocktail
½ cup water
¼ cup ReaLemon® Lemon Juice from Concentrate
Cranberries
Mint leaves, optional

In 1-quart measure or pitcher, combine cranberry juice, water and ReaLemon. Pour *¼ cup* mixture into 1-quart star-shaped mold. Arrange cranberries and leaves in mold. Freeze. Pour remaining liquid over fruit. Freeze.

SCARLETT O'HARA

Makes about 1½ quarts

1 (32-ounce) bottle cranberry juice cocktail, chilled
1 cup Southern Comfort liqueur
⅓ cup ReaLime® Lime Juice from Concentrate
2 to 3 tablespoons sugar
Ice

In pitcher, combine all ingredients except ice; stir until sugar dissolves. Serve over ice. Garnish as desired.

To Make 1 Serving: In cocktail shaker, combine 2 teaspoons confectioners' sugar, ⅓ cup cranberry juice cocktail, 1 jigger (1½ ounces) Southern Comfort liqueur, 1 tablespoon ReaLime and ice; shake well. Strain.

LOW CALORIE LEMONADE

Makes about 1 quart

3¼ cups cold water
½ cup ReaLemon® Lemon Juice from Concentrate
4 to 8 envelopes sugar substitute or 1½ teaspoons liquid sugar substitute

Combine ingredients; mix well. Serve over ice. Garnish as desired.

For 1 serving: Combine ¾ cup cold water, 2 tablespoons ReaLemon and 1 to 2 envelopes sugar substitute or ½ teaspoon liquid sugar substitute.

FROTHY STRAWBERRY
PINEAPPLE PUNCH

Makes about 3½ quarts

1 (46-ounce) can pineapple juice, chilled
½ cup ReaLemon® Lemon Juice from Concentrate
2 (2-quart size) packages un-sweetened strawberry flavor drink mix
¼ cup sugar
2 (32-ounce) bottles ginger ale, chilled
1 quart pineapple sherbet, scooped into balls, *or* pressed into 1-quart ring mold, frozen solid
Fresh strawberries

In large punch bowl, combine pine-apple juice, ReaLemon, drink mix and sugar; stir until sugar dissolves. Just before serving, add ginger ale, sherbet and strawberries.

MULLED CIDER

Makes about 2 quarts

2 quarts apple cider
¾ to 1 cup ReaLemon® Lemon Juice from Concentrate
1 cup firmly packed light brown sugar
8 whole cloves
2 cinnamon sticks
¾ cup rum, optional
Additional cinnamon sticks for garnish, optional

In large saucepan, combine all ingredi-ents except rum and garnish; bring to a boil. Reduce heat; simmer uncovered 10 minutes to blend flavors. Remove spices; add rum just before serving if desired. Serve hot with cinnamon sticks if desired.

Tip: Can be served cold.

MICROWAVE: In deep 3-quart round baking dish, combine ingredients as above. Microwave on full power (high) 13 to 14 minutes or until heated through. Serve as above.

◄ SPARKLING HARVEST CIDER

Makes about 3 quarts

2 quarts apple cider, chilled
1 cup ReaLemon® Lemon Juice from Concentrate
½ cup sugar
1 (32-ounce) bottle ginger ale, chilled
Apple slices or cinnamon sticks, optional
Ice

In punch bowl, combine cider, ReaLemon and sugar; stir until sugar dissolves. Just before serving, add ginger ale. Garnish with apple and cinnamon sticks if desired. Serve over ice.

CHAMPAGNE SHERBET PUNCH ▲

Makes about 2½ quarts

3 cups pineapple juice, chilled
¼ cup ReaLemon® Lemon Juice
from Concentrate
1 quart pineapple sherbet
1 (750 mL) bottle champagne,
chilled

In punch bowl, combine pineapple juice and ReaLemon. Just before serving, scoop sherbet into punch bowl; add champagne. Stir gently.

PLANTER'S PUNCH

Makes about 2½ quarts

4 cups orange juice, chilled
4 cups pineapple juice, chilled
¾ cup ReaLime® Lime Juice from
Concentrate
½ cup grenadine syrup
1½ cups dark rum
Ice

In punch bowl or large pitcher, combine all ingredients except ice; stir. Serve over ice.

FRUIT MEDLEY PUNCH

Makes about 3½ quarts

Della Robbia Ice Ring, optional
2 (10-ounce) packages frozen
strawberries in syrup, partially
thawed
3 cups apricot nectar, chilled
3 cups cold water
1 cup ReaLemon® Lemon Juice
from Concentrate
1 (6-ounce) can frozen orange
juice concentrate, thawed
1 cup sugar
1 (32-ounce) bottle ginger ale,
chilled

Prepare ice ring in advance. In blender container, blend strawberries well. In punch bowl, combine pureed strawberries, apricot nectar, water, ReaLemon, orange juice concentrate and sugar; stir until sugar dissolves. Slowly pour in ginger ale; add Della Robbia Ice Ring if desired.

Della Robbia Ice Ring

2½ cups ginger ale, chilled
½ cup ReaLemon® Lemon Juice
from Concentrate
Canned apricot halves, drained
Seedless green grapes
Strawberries or maraschino
cherries
Strips of orange peel, curled
Mint leaves

In 1-quart measure or pitcher, combine ginger ale and ReaLemon. Pour 2 cups mixture into 1-quart ring mold; freeze. Arrange fruits, peel and mint leaves in mold. Carefully pour remaining liquid over fruit in mold. Freeze.

TOM COLLINS

Makes 1 serving

**2 tablespoons confectioners'
    sugar
1 jigger (1½ ounces) gin or vodka
2 tablespoons ReaLemon® Lemon
    Juice from Concentrate
Ice
Club soda, chilled**

In cocktail shaker, combine sugar, gin
and ReaLemon; shake well. Add ice to
tall glass; pour in gin mixture. Fill with
club soda. Garnish as desired.

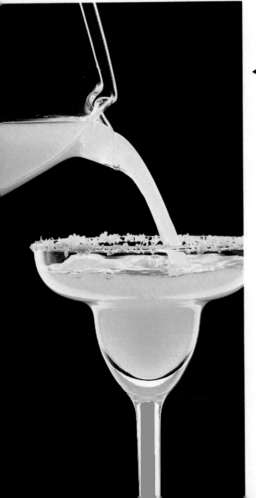

WHISKEY SOUR

Makes 1 serving

**2 tablespoons confectioners'
    sugar
1 jigger (1½ ounces) whiskey,
    bourbon, vodka, scotch or gin
2 tablespoons ReaLemon® Lemon
    Juice from Concentrate
Ice
Maraschino cherry and orange
    slice for garnish optional**

In cocktail shaker, combine all ingredients except garnish in order listed;
shake well. Strain. Garnish with cherry
and orange slice if desired.

To Make 1 Quart: In pitcher, combine
¾ cup confectioner's sugar and ¾ cup
ReaLemon; stir until sugar dissolves.
Add 1 cup liquor and 4 cups ice
cubes; stir.

◀ FROSTY PITCHER MARGARITAS

Makes about 1¾ quarts

**2 (8-ounce) bottles ReaLime®
    Lime Juice from Concentrate,
    chilled
Salt
1 cup confectioners' sugar
4 cups crushed ice
1½ cups tequila
¾ cup triple sec or other orange-
    flavored liqueur**

In saucer, dip rims of cocktail glasses in
1 tablespoon ReaLime; dip in salt. In
blender container, combine remaining
ReaLime with sugar; blend well. Add
ice; blend until slushy. Pour into 2-quart
pitcher; stir in tequila and liqueur.
Serve in prepared glasses.

STRAWBERRY DAIQUIRIS ▲

Makes about 1 quart

- 2 (10-ounce) packages frozen strawberries in syrup, partially thawed
- ½ cup light rum
- ⅓ cup ReaLime® Lime Juice from Concentrate
- ¼ cup confectioners' sugar
- 2 cups ice cubes
  Strawberries for garnish, optional

In blender container, combine all ingredients except ice and garnish; blend well. Gradually add ice, blending until smooth. Garnish with strawberries if desired.

PARTY DAIQUIRIS

Makes about 1½ quarts

- 1 cup sugar
- 2 (8-ounce) bottles ReaLime® Lime Juice from Concentrate, chilled
- 2 cups cold water
- 2 cups light rum
  Crushed ice or ice cubes

In 2-quart pitcher, dissolve sugar in ReaLime; stir in water and rum. Add ice.

PARTY MAI TAIS ▲

Makes about 5 cups

- 3 cups pineapple juice, chilled
- 1 cup light rum
- 1 (6-ounce) can frozen orange juice concentrate, thawed
- ½ cup ReaLemon® Lemon Juice from Concentrate
  Ice
  Orange slices and maraschino cherries for garnish, optional

In pitcher, combine all ingredients except ice and garnish; stir to dissolve orange juice concentrate. Serve over ice; garnish with orange and cherries if desired.

PEACH DAIQUIRIS

Makes about 1 quart

- 2 (10-ounce) packages frozen sliced peaches in syrup, partially thawed
- ½ cup light rum
- ⅓ cup ReaLime® Lime Juice from Concentrate
- ¼ cup confectioners' sugar
- 2 cups ice cubes

In blender container, combine all ingredients except ice; blend well. Gradually add ice, blending until smooth.

◀ PURPLE PASSION

Makes about 4 cups

1 (6-ounce) can frozen sweetened
    grape juice concentrate,
    thawed
3 juice cans cold water
1 juice can vodka
½ cup ReaLemon® Lemon Juice
    from Concentrate
    Ice
    Purple or green grapes and mint
    leaves for garnish, optional

In pitcher, combine all ingredients
except ice and garnish; mix well. Serve
over ice. Garnish with grapes and mint
if desired.

RASPBERRY CHAMPAGNE PUNCH

Makes about 3 quarts

2 (10-ounce) packages frozen red
    raspberries in syrup, thawed
⅓ cup ReaLemon® Lemon Juice
    from Concentrate
½ cup sugar
1 (750 mL) bottle red rosé wine,
    chilled
1 quart raspberry sherbet
1 (750 mL) bottle dry champagne,
    chilled

In blender container, blend raspberries
until smooth. In large punch bowl, combine raspberries, ReaLemon, sugar and
wine; stir until sugar dissolves. Just
before serving, scoop sherbet into punch
bowl; add champagne. Stir gently.

◀ SOUTHERN SUNSHINE

Makes about 7 cups

2 cups orange juice, chilled
½ cup ReaLemon® Lemon Juice
    from Concentrate
¼ cup sugar
¾ cup Southern Comfort liqueur
1 (32-ounce) bottle lemon-lime
    carbonated beverage, chilled
    Ice

In pitcher, combine orange juice,
ReaLemon and sugar; stir until sugar
dissolves. Stir in liqueur and carbonated beverage; serve over ice.
Garnish as desired.

Tip: Recipe can be doubled.

LEMON TODDY

Makes 1 serving

⅓ cup water
¼ cup ReaLemon® Lemon Juice
   from Concentrate
3 tablespoons honey
1 jigger (1½ ounces) whiskey

In small saucepan, combine ingredients. Over low heat, simmer, stirring
occasionally to dissolve honey.
Serve hot.

MICROWAVE: In 1-cup glass measure,
combine ingredients. Microwave on full
power (high) 1 minute or until heated
through, stirring after 30 seconds.
Serve as above.

MINT JULEP COOLER

Makes about 4 cups

¾ cup bourbon
⅓ cup ReaLime® Lime Juice from
   Concentrate
2 tablespoons white creme de
   menthe
2 (12-ounce) cans lemon-lime
   carbonated beverage, chilled
Ice
Mint leaves for garnish, optional

In pitcher, combine bourbon, ReaLime
and creme de menthe. Stir in carbonated beverage; serve over ice.
Garnish with mint if desired.

SYLLABUB

Makes about 5 cups

1 quart half-and-half
½ cup sugar
⅓ cup ReaLemon® Lemon Juice
   from Concentrate, chilled
⅓ cup brandy
3 tablespoons cocktail sherry
Candy lemon sticks for garnish,
   optional

In large mixer bowl, beat half-and-half
on low speed until frothy; gradually
beat in remaining ingredients except
garnish. Pour into glasses; garnish with
lemon sticks if desired.

HOT MAPLE TODDY

Makes about 3 cups

1 to 1¼ cups whiskey
1 cup maple or maple-flavored
   syrup
¾ cup ReaLemon® Lemon Juice
   from Concentrate
Butter and cinnamon sticks,
   optional

In medium saucepan, combine all
ingredients except butter and cinnamon
sticks. Over low heat, simmer to blend
flavors. Serve hot with butter and
cinnamon sticks if desired.

MICROWAVE: In 1-quart glass measure,
combine ingredients as above. Microwave on full power (high) 4 to 5 minutes
or until heated through. Serve as above.

Hot Maple Toddy

BLOODY MARY

Tomato juice, chilled
Vodka
ReaLemon® Lemon Juice from
  Concentrate
Worcestershire sauce
Celery salt
Hot pepper sauce
Pepper

Combine ingredients to make desired amount. Serve over ice; garnish as desired.

To Make:

1 serving
(8 ounces)
	¾ cup tomato juice
	1 jigger (1½ ounces)
	  vodka
	1 teaspoon ReaLemon
	½ teaspoon Worces-
	  tershire sauce
	Dash celery salt
	3 to 5 drops hot
	  pepper sauce
	Dash pepper

1 quart	3 cups tomato juice
	¾ cup vodka
	4 teaspoons
	  ReaLemon
	2 teaspoons Worces-
	  tershire sauce
	½ teaspoon celery salt
	⅛ teaspoon hot
	  pepper sauce
	Dash pepper

2 quarts	1 (46-ounce) can
	  tomato juice
	1½ cups vodka
	3 tablespoons
	  ReaLemon
	4 teaspoons Worces-
	  tershire sauce
	1 teaspoon celery salt
	¼ teaspoon hot
	  pepper sauce
	⅛ teaspoon pepper

Tip: For non-alcoholic Bloody Mary, omit vodka. Proceed as above.

HOT & SPICY BLOODY MARY

Makes about 7 cups

1 (46-ounce) can tomato juice
1 (8-ounce) can tomato sauce
⅓ cup ReaLemon® Lemon Juice
   from Concentrate
5 teaspoons Worcestershire
   sauce
1 tablespoon sugar
1 teaspoon celery salt
½ teaspoon prepared horseradish
9 drops hot pepper sauce
½ cup vodka
   Butter, optional
   Cracked black pepper, optional

In large saucepan, combine all ingredients except vodka, butter and pepper. Bring to a boil; simmer 10 to 15 minutes to blend flavors, stirring occasionally. Just before serving, add vodka. Serve hot with butter and pepper, if desired. Garnish as desired.

BLOODY MARY GARNISHES

Garden Garnish: Dip cucumber spear edge in paprika. Arrange carrot curl on toothpick; insert into cucumber.

Tomato and Frilled Onion: Cut a 1½-inch section from middle of green onion. With small scissors or very sharp knife, make several ½-inch cuts on each end toward center. Chill in ice water until curled. Alternate on toothpick with cherry tomato halves.

Onion & Olive Pick: Dip cocktail onions in chopped parsley; alternate on toothpick with pimiento-stuffed olives.

Green Onion Firecracker: With small scissors or very sharp knife, cut tips of green onion to end of dark green portion. Chill in ice water until curled.

STRAWBERRY WATERMELON SLUSH ▲

Makes about 5 cups

2 cups cubed watermelon
1 pint fresh strawberries,
   cleaned and hulled
½ cup sugar
⅓ cup ReaLemon® Lemon Juice
   from Concentrate
2 cups ice cubes
   Mint leaves, watermelon
   chunks and strawberries for
   garnish, optional

In blender container, combine all
ingredients except ice and garnish;
blend well. Gradually add ice, blending
until smooth. Garnish with mint and
fruit if desired. Serve immediately.

LEMON-LIME SLUSH

Makes about 2 quarts

2 cups water
⅔ cup sugar
⅓ cup ReaLemon® Lemon Juice
   from Concentrate
⅓ cup ReaLime® Lime Juice from
   Concentrate
1 to 1½ cups light rum
1 (32-ounce) bottle lemon-lime
   carbonated beverage

In large bowl, combine water, sugar,
ReaLemon and ReaLime; stir until
sugar dissolves. Add rum and carbonated beverage. Freeze. About 1 hour
before serving, remove from freezer;
when mixture is slushy, spoon into
cocktail glasses. Garnish as desired.

TROPICAL SMOOTHIE

Makes about 2¾ cups

- ¾ cup pineapple juice, chilled
- ½ cup fresh or frozen un-
  sweetened strawberries
- 1 small banana, sliced
- ¼ cup light rum
- ¼ cup ReaLime® Lime Juice from
  Concentrate
- ¼ cup sugar
- 1 cup ice cubes

In blender container, combine all ingredients except ice; blend well. Gradually add ice, blending until smooth. Garnish as desired. Serve immediately.

COCONUT ORANGE FROTH

Makes about 5 cups

- 2 cups orange sherbet
- 1 cup pineapple juice
- ⅓ cup Coco Lopez® Cream of
  Coconut
- ⅓ cup ReaLemon® Lemon Juice
  from Concentrate
- 1 (12-ounce) can club soda,
  chilled

In blender container, combine all ingredients except soda; blend until smooth. Pour into pitcher; add soda. Serve immediately.

BANANA SHAKE

Makes about 5 cups

- 2 ripe bananas, cut up (about
  2 cups)
- ⅓ cup ReaLemon® Lemon Juice
  from Concentrate
- 1 cup cold water
- 1 (14-ounce) can Eagle® Brand
  Sweetened Condensed Milk
  (NOT evaporated milk)
- 2 cups ice cubes

In blender container, combine all ingredients except ice; blend well. Gradually add ice, blending until smooth. Garnish as desired. Refrigerate leftovers. (Mixture stays thick and creamy in refrigerator.)

Mixer Method: In large mixer bowl, mash bananas; gradually beat in ReaLemon, sweetened condensed milk and 2½ cups cold water. Chill before serving.

Strawberry-Banana Shake: Reduce bananas to ½ cup; add 1½ cups fresh strawberries *or* 1 cup frozen un-sweetened strawberries, partially thawed. Proceed as above.

Strawberry-Banana Shake

SPICED TEA

Makes about 1½ quarts

6 cups water
1 cup firmly packed light brown
    sugar
6 cinnamon sticks
8 whole cloves
8 tea bags
1 cup orange juice
½ cup ReaLemon® Lemon Juice
    from Concentrate

In large saucepan, combine water, sugar, cinnamon and cloves; bring to a boil. Reduce heat; simmer uncovered 10 minutes. Remove spices. Pour over tea bags; steep 5 minutes. Remove tea bags; add orange juice and ReaLemon. Serve hot or cold.

ORANGE TEA PUNCH

Makes about 4 quarts

4 cups brewed tea
2 cups orange juice, chilled
1 cup ReaLemon® Lemon Juice
    from Concentrate
1 cup sugar
1 quart orange sherbet
1 (32-ounce) bottle ginger ale,
    chilled

In pitcher, combine tea, orange juice, ReaLemon and sugar; stir until sugar dissolves. Chill. Just before serving, pour tea mixture into large punch bowl; add scoops of sherbet and ginger ale.

LEMON TEA SPARKLER

Makes about 7 cups

2 cups brewed tea
½ cup ReaLemon® Lemon Juice
    from Concentrate
½ cup sugar
1 (32-ounce) bottle ginger ale,
    chilled
    Ice

In pitcher, combine tea, ReaLemon and sugar; stir until sugar dissolves. Just before serving, add ginger ale. Serve over ice.

◀ LEMONY ICED TEA

Makes about 7 cups

6 cups brewed tea
½ cup ReaLemon® Lemon Juice
    from Concentrate
¾ cup sugar
    Ice

In pitcher, combine tea, ReaLemon and sugar; stir until sugar dissolves. Chill if desired. Serve over ice.

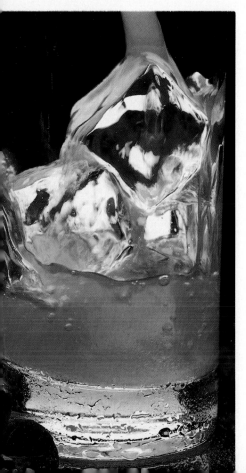

PINEAPPLE TEA ▶

Makes about 2 quarts

2 tablespoons unsweetened instant tea
½ cup sugar
1 cup hot water
4 cups pineapple juice, chilled
1½ cups cold water
¾ cup ReaLemon® Lemon Juice from Concentrate
Ice
Pineapple chunks, maraschino cherries and mint leaves for garnish, optional

In pitcher, combine tea and sugar; add hot water. Stir until sugar dissolves. Add pineapple juice, cold water and ReaLemon; serve over ice. Garnish with fruit and mint if desired.

GOLDEN CITRUS PUNCH

Makes about 2 quarts

3 cups orange juice, chilled
2 cups brewed tea
½ cup ReaLemon® Lemon Juice from Concentrate
1 cup sugar
1 (750 mL) bottle sauterne, chilled
¼ cup orange-flavored liqueur
Ice block or ice ring
Orange slices

In small punch bowl, combine orange juice, tea, ReaLemon and sugar; stir until sugar dissolves. Chill. Add sauterne and liqueur. Add ice; garnish with orange slices.

Fish & Seafood

Add lively lemon flavor to your favorite fish dishes and succulent seafood with ReaLemon. Create a sensation with our Shrimp Curry or Stir-Fried Scallops and Vegetables. Please the family with Creole Tuna Loaf or easy Chipper-Cheese Fish.

QUICK TARTAR SAUCE

Makes about 1 cup

- ¾ cup mayonnaise or salad dressing
- 2 tablespoons pickle relish, drained
- 1 tablespoon chopped green onion
- 1 tablespoon ReaLemon® Lemon Juice from Concentrate

In small bowl, combine ingredients; mix well. Chill to blend flavors.

TANGY COCKTAIL SAUCE

Makes about 1 cup

- ¾ cup chili sauce or catsup
- 3 tablespoons ReaLemon® Lemon Juice from Concentrate
- ½ teaspoon prepared horseradish
- ½ teaspoon Worcestershire sauce

In small bowl, combine ingredients. Chill to blend flavors.

LEMON BUTTER SAUCE

Makes about ⅔ cup

- ½ cup margarine or butter
- 3 tablespoons ReaLemon® Lemon Juice from Concentrate
- ⅛ teaspoon salt

In small saucepan, melt margarine; stir in ReaLemon and salt. Serve with fish, seafood or vegetables.

BEER BATTER FISH

Makes 4 servings

1½ cups Homemade Batter Mix*
1 pound fish fillets, fresh or
    frozen, thawed
⅓ cup ReaLemon® Lemon Juice
    from Concentrate
⅔ cup beer
    Vegetable oil

Prepare Batter Mix. Pat fish dry. Coat fish with ½ cup Batter Mix. In large bowl, combine remaining mix, ReaLemon and beer; mix well. Dip fish into batter. Fry in hot oil until golden brown; drain. Serve immediately with additional ReaLemon. Refrigerate leftovers.

*Homemade Batter Mix: Combine 1½ cups unsifted flour, 2¼ teaspoons baking powder, 1 teaspoon salt and ¾ teaspoon baking soda; mix well.

DILLED LEMON FISH

Makes 4 servings

¼ cup ReaLemon® Lemon Juice
    from Concentrate
¼ cup water
2 tablespoons margarine or
    butter
1 teaspoon Wyler's® Chicken-
    Flavor Instant Bouillon
¼ teaspoon dill weed or thyme
    leaves
1 pound fish fillets, fresh or
    frozen, thawed

In large skillet, combine ReaLemon, water, margarine, bouillon and dill; heat until bouillon dissolves. Add fish; cover and simmer 6 to 8 minutes or until fish flakes with fork. Garnish with paprika if desired. Refrigerate leftovers.

MICROWAVE: In 12x7-inch baking dish, combine all ingredients except fish; microwave on full power (high) 6 minutes or until bouillon dissolves, stirring after 3 and 6 minutes. Add fish; cover with plastic wrap. Microwave on full power (high) 5 to 6 minutes or until fish flakes with fork. Serve as above.

LEMON BATTER FISH

Makes 4 servings

1 cup unsifted flour
⅔ cup water
⅓ cup ReaLemon® Lemon Juice
    from Concentrate
1 egg, beaten
1 teaspoon baking powder
¾ teaspoon salt
½ teaspoon sugar
1 pound fish fillets, fresh or
    frozen, thawed
    Additional ReaLemon® Lemon
    Juice from Concentrate
    Flour
    Vegetable oil

In medium bowl, mix *1 cup* flour, water, *⅓ cup* ReaLemon, egg, baking powder, salt and sugar. Dip fish in additional ReaLemon; coat with flour then batter. Fry in hot oil until golden brown; drain. Serve immediately. Refrigerate leftovers.

Tip: Use Lemon Batter to coat shrimp, scallops or oysters. Proceed as above; omit dipping seafood in ReaLemon.

LIVELY LEMON ROLL-UPS ▶

Makes 8 servings

1 cup cooked rice
⅓ cup margarine or butter
⅓ cup ReaLemon® Lemon Juice
    from Concentrate
2 teaspoons salt
¼ teaspoon pepper
1 (10-ounce) package frozen
    chopped broccoli, thawed
    and well drained
1 cup (4 ounces) shredded
    Cheddar cheese
8 fish fillets, fresh or frozen,
    thawed (about 2 pounds)
    Paprika

Preheat oven to 375°. In small saucepan, melt margarine; add ReaLemon,
salt and pepper. In medium bowl,
combine rice, broccoli, cheese and ¼
cup ReaLemon sauce; mix well. Divide
broccoli mixture equally among fillets.
Roll up and place seam-side down in
shallow 2-quart baking dish. Pour
remaining sauce over roll-ups. Bake 25
minutes or until fish flakes with fork.
Spoon sauce over individual servings;
garnish with paprika. Refrigerate
leftovers.

MICROWAVE: Prepare fish as above.
Arrange in 12x7-inch baking dish;
cover with plastic wrap. Microwave on
full power (high) 10 to 12 minutes or
until fish flakes with fork, rotating dish
once. Serve as above.

PARSLEY BUTTER SAUCE

Makes about ⅔ cup

½ cup margarine or butter
3 tablespoons ReaLemon® Lemon
    Juice from Concentrate
1 tablespoon chopped parsley
⅛ teaspoon salt

In small saucepan, melt margarine; stir
in ReaLemon, parsley and salt. Serve
with fish, seafood or vegetables.

Herb Lemon: Omit parsley. Add 1
teaspoon oregano leaves or dill weed.

Lemon Garlic: Omit salt. Add ¼ teaspoon
garlic salt.

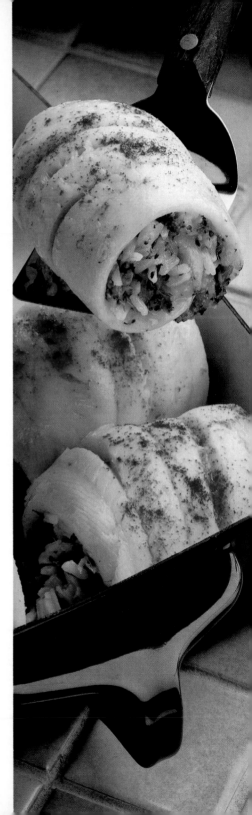

MARINATED BAKED FISH ▲

Makes 2 to 4 servings

¼ cup margarine or butter, melted
¼ cup ReaLemon® Lemon Juice
   from Concentrate
¼ cup sliced green onions
2 tablespoons water
½ teaspoon garlic salt
¼ to ½ teaspoon dill weed
1 pound salmon or halibut
   steaks, fresh or frozen,
   thawed

In 12x7-inch baking dish, combine all
ingredients except fish. Add fish;
marinate 1 hour. Bake fish in marinade
in preheated 350° oven 15 to 20
minutes or until fish flakes with fork.
Garnish as desired. Refrigerate leftovers.

MICROWAVE: Prepare fish as above,
marinating in 12x7-inch baking dish.
Cover with plastic wrap; microwave fish
in marinade on full power (high) 5 to 7
minutes or until fish flakes with fork.
Serve as above.

SAVORY SKILLET FISH

Makes 4 servings

½ cup water
¼ cup margarine or butter
¼ cup ReaLemon® Lemon Juice
   from Concentrate
2 teaspoons Wyler's® Chicken-
   Flavor Instant Bouillon
½ cup thinly sliced carrots
½ cup chopped celery
½ cup chopped green pepper
½ cup chopped onion
1 pound fish fillets, fresh or
   frozen, thawed

In large skillet, combine water, margarine, ReaLemon and bouillon; heat
until bouillon dissolves. Add vegetables;
cover and simmer 10 minutes. Add fish;
cover and simmer 10 to 15 minutes or
until fish flakes with fork. Refrigerate
leftovers.

MICROWAVE: In 12x7-inch baking
dish, combine all ingredients except
fish; cover with plastic wrap. Microwave
on full power (high) 10 to 12 minutes or
until mixture boils. Add fish fillets;
microwave on full power (high) 2 to 3
minutes until fish flakes with fork. Let
stand 5 minutes before serving.

GRILLED FISH IN FOIL

Makes 4 servings

1 pound fish fillets, fresh or
   frozen, thawed
2 tablespoons margarine or
   butter
¼ cup ReaLemon® Lemon Juice
   from Concentrate
1 tablespoon chopped parsley
1 teaspoon dill weed
1 teaspoon salt
¼ teaspoon pepper
   Paprika
1 medium onion, thinly sliced

On 4 large buttered squares of heavy-
duty aluminum foil, place equal amounts
of fish. In small saucepan, melt margarine; add ReaLemon, parsley, dill
weed, salt and pepper. Pour equal
amounts over fish. Sprinkle with
paprika; top with onion slices. Wrap foil
securely around fish, leaving space for
fish to expand. Grill 5 to 7 minutes on
each side or until fish flakes with fork.
Refrigerate leftovers.

SWEET AND SOUR SHRIMP ▲

Makes 4 servings

1 pound medium raw shrimp,
   peeled and deveined
1 (20-ounce) can pineapple
   chunks in juice, drained,
   reserving juice
¾ cup cold water
⅓ cup ReaLemon® Lemon Juice
   from Concentrate
⅓ cup firmly packed light brown
   sugar
3 tablespoons cornstarch
3 tablespoons soy sauce
⅛ teaspoon ground ginger
1 (8-ounce) can sliced water
   chestnuts, drained
1 green pepper, cut into chunks
   Hot cooked rice

In large skillet, combine reserved
pineapple juice, water, ReaLemon,
sugar, cornstarch, soy sauce and
ginger. Over medium heat, cook and
stir until thick and clear. Add shrimp;
cook 3 minutes. Add remaining ingredients; heat through. Serve with rice.
Refrigerate leftovers.

51

CREOLE TUNA LOAF

Makes 6 to 8 servings

2 (12½-ounce) cans tuna,
   drained and flaked
2½ cups fresh bread crumbs
   (about 4 slices)
½ cup mayonnaise or salad
   dressing
¼ cup chopped celery
¼ cup chopped green pepper
¼ cup chopped onion
3 tablespoons ReaLemon®
   Lemon Juice from
   Concentrate
2 eggs
   Creole Sauce

Preheat oven to 350°. In large bowl,
combine all ingredients except Creole
Sauce. In greased shallow baking dish,
shape into loaf. Bake 35 to 40 minutes
or until golden brown. Serve with
Creole Sauce. Refrigerate leftovers.

MICROWAVE: Mix ingredients as
above. Turn into 2½-quart microwave
baking ring. Microwave on full power
(high) 12 to 13 minutes or until set and
almost firm in center. Let stand 5
minutes. Serve as above.

Creole Sauce

1 (15-ounce) can stewed tomatoes
2 teaspoons cornstarch
3 tablespoons ReaLemon®
   Lemon Juice from
   Concentrate
1 teaspoon Worcestershire sauce
¾ teaspoon sugar
⅛ teaspoon hot pepper sauce

In small saucepan, combine tomatoes
and cornstarch; mix well. Add remaining ingredients. Over high heat, bring
to a boil. Reduce heat; continue
cooking 5 minutes. (Makes about
2 cups)

MICROWAVE: In 1-quart glass measure,
combine tomatoes and cornstarch. Add
remaining ingredients. Microwave on
full power (high) 8 minutes or until
thickened, stirring every 2 minutes.

DILLY SALMON LOAF

Makes 4 to 6 servings

1 (15½-ounce) can salmon,
  drained and flaked
2 cups fresh bread crumbs
  (about 4 slices)
2 eggs, beaten
¼ cup finely chopped onion
3 tablespoons margarine or
  butter, melted
2 tablespoons ReaLemon®
  Lemon Juice from
  Concentrate
½ teaspoon salt
¼ teaspoon dill weed
  Lemony Dill Sauce

Preheat oven to 350°. In large bowl,
combine all ingredients except Lemony
Dill Sauce; mix well. In greased shallow
baking dish, shape into loaf. Bake 35 to
40 minutes. Let stand 5 minutes before
serving. Serve with Lemony Dill Sauce;
garnish as desired. Refrigerate leftovers.

Lemony Dill Sauce

⅓ cup margarine or butter
¾ cup mayonnaise or salad
  dressing
1 egg
¼ cup ReaLemon® Lemon Juice
  from Concentrate
2 tablespoons water
1 tablespoon sugar
1 teaspoon Wyler's® Chicken-
  Flavor Instant Bouillon
¼ teaspoon dill weed

In small saucepan, melt margarine. Add
mayonnaise, egg, ReaLemon, water,
sugar, bouillon and dill; mix well. Over
low heat, cook and stir until thickened
(do not boil). Refrigerate leftovers.
(Makes about 1½ cups)

SHRIMP CURRY

Makes 6 to 8 servings

2 pounds raw shrimp, peeled and
   deveined
1 cup chopped onion
¼ cup margarine or butter
¼ cup unsifted flour
2½ cups milk or half-and-half
¾ cup Coco Lopez® Cream of
   Coconut
1 tablespoon curry powder
1 teaspoon salt
½ teaspoon ground ginger
¼ cup ReaLemon® Lemon Juice
   from Concentrate *or*
   ReaLime® Lime Juice from
   Concentrate

In large skillet, cook onion in margarine until tender; stir in flour. Gradually add milk; stir until smooth. Add cream of coconut, curry, salt and ginger. Over medium heat, cook and stir until thickened. Add ReaLemon. Reduce heat; simmer uncovered 20 minutes, stirring occasionally. Add shrimp. Over medium heat, cook 10 to 15 minutes, stirring occasionally. Serve with rice and condiments. Refrigerate leftovers.

Condiments: Toasted coconut, sunflower meats, peanuts, green onions, hard-cooked eggs, chutney, crumbled bacon or raisins.

STIR-FRIED SCALLOPS & VEGETABLES

Makes 4 servings

1 pound scallops
¼ cup ReaLemon® Lemon Juice
  from Concentrate
1 cup thinly sliced carrots
3 cloves garlic, finely chopped
⅓ cup margarine or butter
2 cups sliced fresh mushrooms
  (about 8 ounces)
¾ teaspoon thyme leaves
2 teaspoons cornstarch
½ teaspoon salt
¼ cup diagonally sliced green
  onions
1 (6-ounce) package frozen pea
  pods, thawed, or 4 ounces
  fresh pea pods
2 tablespoons dry sherry
  Hot cooked rice

In shallow baking dish, marinate scallops in ReaLemon 30 minutes, stirring occasionally. In large skillet, over high heat, cook and stir carrots and garlic in margarine until tender-crisp, about 3 minutes. Add mushrooms and thyme; cook and stir about 5 minutes. Stir cornstarch and salt into scallop mixture; add to vegetables. Cook and stir until scallops are opaque, about 4 minutes. Stir in onions, pea pods and sherry. Remove from heat. Serve immediately with hot cooked rice. Refrigerate leftovers.

SKILLET FISH ITALIANO

Makes 4 servings

- 1 small onion, sliced
- 2 tablespoons margarine or butter
- 1 pound fish fillets, fresh or frozen, thawed
- ¼ cup ReaLemon® Lemon Juice from Concentrate
- ½ teaspoon oregano leaves
- 2 cups sliced zucchini
- 1 cup sliced fresh mushrooms (about 4 ounces)
- ½ cup chopped tomato
- ½ cup (2 ounces) shredded Swiss cheese

In large skillet, cook onion in margarine until tender. Add fish, ReaLemon, oregano, zucchini and mushrooms; cover and simmer 10 minutes. Top with tomato and cheese; cover and simmer 2 minutes or until cheese melts. Serve immediately. Refrigerate leftovers.

LINGUINE WITH LEMON CLAM SAUCE

Makes 2 to 3 servings

- 1 clove garlic, finely chopped
- 2 tablespoons margarine or butter
- 2 tablespoons vegetable oil
- 2 (6½-ounce) cans Snow's® Chopped Clams, drained, reserving ⅔ cup liquid
- ¼ cup chopped onion
- 2 tablespoons ReaLemon® Lemon Juice from Concentrate
- ½ teaspoon cracked black pepper
- 1 bay leaf
- 1 tablespoon chopped parsley
  Hot cooked linguine
  Grated Parmesan cheese

In medium skillet, cook garlic in margarine and oil until golden. Add reserved clam liquid, onion, ReaLemon, pepper and bay leaf. Bring to a boil; simmer uncovered 5 minutes. Stir in clams and parsley; heat through. Remove bay leaf; serve with hot linguine, cheese and additional cracked black pepper. Refrigerate leftovers.

Skillet Fish Italiano

CHIPPER-CHEESE FISH

Makes 4 servings

- 3 tablespoons margarine or butter, melted
- 2 tablespoons ReaLemon® Lemon Juice from Concentrate
- 1½ cups crushed potato chips
- ¼ cup grated Parmesan cheese
- ½ teaspoon oregano leaves, optional
- 1 pound fish fillets, fresh or frozen, thawed

Preheat oven to 350°. In greased 13x9-inch baking dish, melt margarine; stir in ReaLemon. In medium bowl, combine chips, cheese and oregano; set aside. Dip fish in ReaLemon mixture, then in chip mixture; arrange in baking dish. Top with remaining chips. Bake 20 to 25 minutes or until fish flakes with fork. Refrigerate leftovers.

SHRIMP & SCALLOP KABOBS

Makes 6 to 8 servings

- 1 pound large raw shrimp, peeled and deveined
- 1 pound sea scallops, cut in half
- ½ cup vegetable oil
- ¼ cup ReaLemon® Lemon Juice from Concentrate
- ¼ cup soy sauce
- 2 cloves garlic, finely chopped
- 2 tablespoons chopped crystalized ginger or 1½ teaspoons ground ginger
- 1 teaspoon onion powder
- 1 (16-ounce) can pineapple chunks, drained
- 2 small zucchini, sliced

In medium bowl, combine oil, ReaLemon, soy sauce, garlic, ginger and onion powder; mix well. Add shrimp and scallops. Cover; refrigerate 3 hours or overnight. Place shrimp, scallops, pineapple and zucchini on skewers. Grill or broil 3 to 6 minutes per side or until shrimp are pink, basting frequently with marinade. Refrigerate leftovers.

Meats & Poultry

Use ReaLemon for savory marinades to tenderize meats and add extra flavor to barbecue sauces and glazes. Complement all kinds of chicken creations— baked, roasted, grilled, stir-fried—with the tantalizing taste of ReaLemon.

SOY MARINADE

Makes about 1½ cups

**½ cup ReaLemon® Lemon Juice
  from Concentrate
½ cup soy sauce
½ cup vegetable oil
3 tablespoons catsup
3 to 4 cloves garlic, finely
  chopped
¼ teaspoon pepper**

In small bowl, combine ingredients. Pour over meat or poultry. Refrigerate 6 hours or overnight, turning occasionally. Remove meat from marinade; grill or broil as desired, basting frequently with marinade.

TERIYAKI MARINADE

Makes about 1 cup

**⅓ cup ReaLemon® Lemon Juice
  from Concentrate
¼ cup soy sauce
¼ cup vegetable oil
3 tablespoons chili sauce
2 cloves garlic, finely chopped
½ teaspoon ground ginger
¼ teaspoon pepper**

In small bowl, combine ingredients. Pour over meat or poultry. Refrigerate 6 hours or overnight, turning occasionally. Remove meat from marinade; grill or broil as desired, basting frequently with marinade.

Pictured: Lemony Glazed and Stuffed Chicken (recipe page 70), Steak with Soy Marinade.

59

HURRY-UP HAM GLAZE

Makes about 1 cup, enough to glaze a large ham

1 cup firmly packed brown sugar
¼ cup ReaLemon® Lemon Juice from Concentrate
¼ cup honey
1 teaspoon dry mustard

In small saucepan, combine ingredients; bring to a boil. Use to baste ham frequently during last 30 minutes of baking.

MICROWAVE: In 1-quart glass measure, combine ingredients. Microwave on full power (high) 2½ to 3 minutes, or until mixture comes to a boil, stirring every minute. Proceed as above.

CANDY APPLE HAM GLAZE ▼

Makes about 1 cup, enough to glaze a large ham

½ cup apple jelly
½ cup red cinnamon candies
¼ cup ReaLemon® Lemon Juice from Concentrate

In small heavy saucepan, combine ingredients. Over medium low heat, cook and stir until candies are completely melted. Use to baste ham frequently during last 30 minutes of baking.

Continued next column

Candy Apple Ham Glaze

MICROWAVE: In 1-quart glass measure, combine ingredients. Microwave on full power (high) 8 to 9 minutes or until candies are completely melted, stirring every 2 minutes. Proceed as above.

MARINATED LAMB SHANKS

Makes 4 servings

⅓ cup ReaLemon® Lemon Juice from Concentrate
1 (0.7-ounce) package Italian salad dressing mix
⅓ cup plus ¼ cup vegetable oil
4 lamb shanks (about ¾ pound each)
⅓ cup plus 1 tablespoon unsifted flour
½ teaspoon salt
8 small whole onions
4 medium carrots, pared and halved
¾ cup water

To make marinade, in 1-pint jar with tight-fitting lid or cruet, combine ReaLemon, salad dressing mix and *⅓ cup* oil; shake well. Place meat in shallow baking dish; pour marinade over. Cover; refrigerate 5 hours or overnight, turning occasionally. Remove meat from dish, reserving marinade. Combine *⅓ cup* flour and salt; coat meat. In Dutch oven or large skillet, brown meat in remaining *¼ cup* oil; pour off fat. Pour reserved marinade over meat; cover and simmer 2 hours. Add vegetables; cook 30 minutes longer or until tender. Remove meat and vegetables from pan; pour off fat, reserving drippings in pan. To make gravy, mix remaining *1 tablespoon* flour with *2 tablespoons* water until smooth; add remaining water. Stir into drippings; cook and stir until thickened. Serve with meat and vegetables. Refrigerate leftovers.

GLAZED MEAT LOAF

Makes 4 to 6 servings

- ½ cup catsup
- ⅓ cup firmly packed light brown sugar
- ¼ cup ReaLemon® Lemon Juice from Concentrate
- 1 teaspoon dry mustard
- 1½ pounds lean ground beef
- 1½ cups fresh bread crumbs (about 2½ slices)
- ¼ cup finely chopped onion
- 1 egg, slightly beaten
- 1 teaspoon Wyler's® Beef-Flavor Instant Bouillon

Preheat oven to 350°. In small bowl, combine catsup, sugar, *1 tablespoon* ReaLemon and mustard; set aside. In large bowl, combine remaining ingredients and *⅓ cup* sauce; mix well. In shallow baking dish, shape into loaf. Bake 1 hour; pour off fat. Pour remaining sauce over top of meat loaf; continue baking 10 minutes. Garnish as desired. Refrigerate leftovers.

MICROWAVE: Mix and shape loaf as above. Cover with wax paper. Microwave on full power (high) 13 to 15 minutes, rotating dish after 8 minutes. Pour remaining sauce over meat loaf; microwave on full power (high) 3 minutes or until center of loaf is firm. Cover with aluminum foil; let stand 5 minutes before serving.

BARBECUE BEEF SANDWICHES

Makes about 30 servings

1½ cups water
1¼ cups catsup
¾ cup chopped onion
½ cup firmly packed brown sugar
⅓ cup chopped celery
¼ cup ReaLemon® Lemon Juice from Concentrate
2 teaspoons chili powder
1 teaspoon salt
½ teaspoon pepper
¼ teaspoon hot pepper sauce
4 pounds beef stew cubes

Preheat oven to 350°. In Dutch oven, combine all ingredients except meat; mix well. Add meat. Over high heat, bring to a boil. Cover; bake 3 hours or until tender. Break meat into small pieces. Serve in pita bread or on buns. Refrigerate leftovers.

Range Top Method: Combine ingredients as above. Bring to a boil; reduce heat. Cover; simmer 3 hours or until tender. Proceed as above.

SALSA

Makes about 1½ cups

¼ cup chopped onion
1 tablespoon margarine or butter
1 (8-ounce) can tomato sauce
1 (3-ounce) can chopped green chilies, drained
2 tablespoons ReaLime® Lime Juice from Concentrate
½ teaspoon sugar
¼ teaspoon oregano leaves
⅛ teaspoon garlic powder
⅛ teaspoon ground cumin
½ cup seeded and chopped tomatoes

In small saucepan, cook onion in margarine until tender. Stir in remaining ingredients except tomatoes. Simmer uncovered 10 minutes; stir in tomatoes. Serve warm with hamburgers, fish, tacos, tostadas or tortilla chips. Refrigerate leftovers.

Barbecue Ham

MARINATED FRENCH DIP

Makes 6 to 8 servings

2 cups water
**⅓ cup ReaLemon® Lemon Juice
from Concentrate**
⅓ cup soy sauce
1 medium onion, thinly sliced
**2 teaspoons Wyler's® Beef-
Flavor Instant Bouillon**
1 teaspoon thyme leaves
2 cloves garlic, finely chopped
**1 (2-pound) beef brisket, pierced
French bread or rolls**

In shallow baking dish, combine all
ingredients except meat and bread; mix
well. Add meat; cover. Refrigerate 6
hours or overnight, turning occasionally.
Cover; bake at 325° for 1 hour and 30
to 45 minutes or until tender, turning
after 45 minutes. Remove meat from
baking dish; reserve marinade. Slice
meat; serve on bread with marinade.
Refrigerate leftovers.

BARBECUE HAM SANDWICHES

Makes 6 to 8 sandwiches

1 cup catsup
**3 tablespoons ReaLemon®
Lemon Juice from
Concentrate**
¼ cup chopped onion
¼ cup firmly packed brown sugar
**2 tablespoons Worcestershire
sauce**
1 teaspon prepared mustard
**1 pound thinly sliced ham
Buns or hard rolls**

In small saucepan, combine all ingredients except ham and buns. Simmer
uncovered 5 minutes. Add ham; heat
through. Serve on buns. Refrigerate
leftovers.

MICROWAVE: In 2-quart round baking
dish, combine ingredients as above.
Cover with wax paper; microwave on
full power (high) 3 minutes. Stir in ham;
cover with wax paper and microwave
on full power (high) 3 to 4 minutes or
until hot. Serve as above.

LIME KABOBS POLYNESIAN

Makes 6 servings

½ cup ReaLime® Lime Juice from
   Concentrate
½ cup vegetable oil
3 tablespoons sugar
1 tablespoon chili sauce
½ to 1 teaspoon curry powder
¼ teaspoon garlic powder
1 (1½-pound) sirloin steak (about
   1-inch thick), cut into cubes
1 (8-ounce) can pineapple
   chunks, drained
1 large green pepper, cut into bite-
   size pieces
2 medium onions, quartered and
   separated into bite-size
   pieces
8 ounces fresh whole mushrooms
   (about 2 cups)
½ pint cherry tomatoes
   Hot cooked rice

In 1-pint jar with tight-fitting lid or cruet,
combine ReaLime, oil, sugar, chili
sauce, curry and garlic powder; shake
well. In large shallow baking dish, pour
marinade over meat. Cover; refrigerate
6 hours or overnight, stirring occasionally. Skewer meat with pineapple and
vegetables. Grill or broil as desired,
basting frequently with marinade.
Serve with rice. Refrigerate leftovers.

MICROWAVE PRE-COOKING
BRATWURST

Pierce 1 pound bratwursts several times
with fork. Arrange in 10x6-inch baking
dish; add 2 teaspoons water. Cover with
plastic wrap; microwave on full power
(high) 5 minutes. Broil, fry or grill
as desired.

ZESTY BARBECUED RIBS

Makes 6 to 8 servings

6 pounds spareribs
Water
2 cups catsup
½ cup ReaLemon® Lemon Juice
from Concentrate
½ cup firmly packed brown sugar
1 tablespoon prepared mustard
½ cup finely chopped onion
¼ cup margarine or butter
¼ cup Worcestershire sauce
1 clove garlic, finely chopped
¼ teaspoon salt
⅛ teaspoon hot pepper sauce

In large pan, cook ribs in boiling water 45 to 60 minutes or until tender. Meanwhile, in medium saucepan, combine remaining ingredients; simmer uncovered 20 minutes, stirring occasionally. Grill or broil ribs as desired, turning and basting frequently with sauce. Refrigerate leftovers.

MICROWAVE: To pre-cook ribs, place 1½-pounds ribs in 12x7-inch shallow baking dish. Add ¼ cup water; cover with vented plastic wrap. Microwave on full power (high) 5 minutes. Reduce to ½ power (medium); continue cooking 7 minutes. Turn ribs over; cook covered on ½ power (medium) 7 minutes longer. Repeat with remaining ribs. Proceed as above.

Zesty Barbecued Ribs

QUICK BARBECUE SAUCE

Makes about 1 cup

¼ cup finely chopped onion
1 clove garlic, finely chopped
2 tablespoons margarine or
butter
1 cup catsup
¼ cup firmly packed brown sugar
¼ cup ReaLemon® Lemon Juice
from Concentrate
1 tablespoon Worcestershire
sauce
1 teaspoon prepared mustard
⅛ teaspoon hot pepper sauce

In small saucepan, cook onion and garlic in margarine until tender. Add remaining ingredients; bring to a boil. Reduce heat; simmer uncovered 15 to 20 minutes. Use as basting sauce for pork, chicken or beef. Refrigerate leftovers.

MICROWAVE: In 1-quart glass measure, microwave margarine on full power (high) 30 to 45 seconds or until melted. Add onion and garlic. Microwave on full power (high) 1½ to 2 minutes or until tender. Add remaining ingredients; cover with wax paper. Microwave on full power (high) 3 to 5 minutes or until mixture boils. Microwave on ⅔ power (medium-high) 4 to 5 minutes to blend flavors. Proceed as above.

◀CRANBERRY GLAZED PORK ROAST

Makes 10 to 12 servings

**1 (3½- to 4-pound) boneless pork
loin roast
Salt and pepper
1 (16-ounce) can whole berry
cranberry sauce
¼ cup ReaLemon® Lemon Juice
from Concentrate
3 tablespoons brown sugar
1 teaspoon cornstarch**

Preheat oven to 450°. Place meat in shallow baking dish; season with salt and pepper. Roast 20 minutes. Reduce oven temperature to 325°; continue roasting. Meanwhile, in small saucepan, combine remaining ingredients. Over medium heat, cook and stir until slightly thickened and clear, about 5 minutes. After meat has cooked 1 hour, drain off fat; spoon half of sauce over meat. Continue roasting 1 to 1½ hours or until meat thermometer reaches 170°, basting occasionally. Spoon remaining sauce over meat; return to oven 10 to 15 minutes. Let stand 10 minutes before slicing. Refrigerate leftovers.

To Make Gravy: In small saucepan, combine meat drippings and 2 tablespoons cornstarch. Over medium heat, cook and stir until thickened and clear, about 5 minutes. (Makes about 2 cups)

EASY PEACH GLAZE

Makes about 1 cup

**1 (12-ounce) jar apricot or peach
preserves (1 cup)
2 tablespoons ReaLemon®
Lemon Juice from
Concentrate
1 tablespoon margarine or butter**

In small saucepan, combine ingredients; mix well. Bring to a boil. Reduce heat; simmer uncovered 10 to 15 minutes to blend flavors. Use to glaze ham loaf, ham, chicken, pork, carrots or sweet potatoes.

MICROWAVE PRE-COOKING CHICKEN

Arrange 3 pounds broiler-fryer chicken parts in 12x7-inch baking dish. Cover with plastic wrap. Microwave on full power (high) 10 minutes, rearranging after 5 minutes. Broil or grill as desired.

SWEET AND SOUR PORK CHOPS

Makes 6 servings

6 center cut pork chops (about 1¾ pounds)
Vegetable oil
½ cup ReaLemon® Lemon Juice from Concentrate
3 tablespoons cornstarch
½ cup firmly packed brown sugar
¼ cup chopped onion
1 tablespoon soy sauce
1 teaspoon Wyler's® Chicken-Flavor Instant Bouillon *or* 1 Chicken-Flavor Bouillon Cube
1 (20-ounce) can pineapple chunks in heavy syrup, drained, reserving syrup
1 cup thinly sliced carrots
Green pepper rings
Hot cooked rice

Preheat oven to 350°. In large oven-proof skillet, brown chops in oil. Remove chops from skillet; pour off fat. In skillet, combine ReaLemon and cornstarch; mix well. Add sugar, onion, soy sauce, bouillon and reserved syrup; cook and stir until slightly thickened and bouillon is dissolved. Add pork chops and carrots. Cover; bake 1 hour or until tender. Add pineapple; cover and bake 10 minutes longer. Garnish with green pepper; serve with rice. Refrigerate leftovers.

LAMB CHOPS WITH LEMONY APPLE GLAZE

Makes 4 servings

½ cup apple jelly
¼ cup ReaLemon® Lemon Juice from Concentrate
¼ cup steak sauce
8 loin lamb chops, 1-inch thick
Salt and pepper

In small saucepan, melt jelly; stir in ReaLemon and steak sauce. Heat through. Grill or broil as desired, basting frequently with sauce. Refrigerate leftovers.

GLAZED HAM STEAK

Makes 4 servings

1 (8-ounce) can crushed pineapple, well drained
½ cup peach or apricot preserves
2 tablespoons ReaLemon® Lemon Juice from Concentrate
1 teaspoon cornstarch
1 (1- to 1½-pound) center cut ham slice

In small saucepan, combine pineapple, preserves, ReaLemon and cornstarch; bring to a boil. Reduce heat; simmer uncovered 10 to 15 minutes to blend flavors. Broil ham to desired doneness on both sides; spoon pineapple mixture on top; heat until hot and bubbly. Refrigerate leftovers.

Sweet and Sour Pork Chops

SIMPLE SAUERBRATEN

Makes 8 to 10 servings

2 medium onions, sliced
2 medium carrots, sliced
2 bay leaves
1 teaspoon peppercorns
2½ cups water
1 cup ReaLemon® Lemon Juice from Concentrate
½ cup sugar
1 (4-pound) rolled beef rump roast
2 tablespoons vegetable oil
12 gingersnap cookies, crushed

In large saucepan, combine all ingredients except meat, oil and cookies; heat. Place meat in large bowl; pour hot marinade over meat. Cover; refrigerate 1 to 3 days, turning meat occasionally. Reserving marinade, remove meat and pat dry. In Dutch oven, brown meat in oil. Add marinade; cover and simmer 2 hours or until tender. Remove meat; strain marinade, reserving 2½ cups liquid. In medium saucepan, combine reserved liquid and cookies; cook and stir until thickened. Serve with meat. Refrigerate leftovers.

VERSATILE MARINADE

Makes about 1 cup

½ cup ReaLemon® Lemon Juice from Concentrate
½ cup vegetable oil
2 cloves garlic, finely chopped
1 teaspoon salt
¼ teaspoon pepper
½ teaspoon herb*

In small bowl, combine ingredients. Pour over lamb, pork or chicken. Refrigerate 6 hours or overnight, turning occasionally. Remove meat from marinade; grill or broil as desired, basting frequently with marinade.

*Herb: Rosemary leaves with lamb
Thyme leaves with pork
Tarragon leaves with chicken

WHISKEY SOUR SIRLOIN

Makes 6 to 8 servings

1 (3-pound) round-bone sirloin steak, 2-inches thick
⅓ cup ReaLemon® Lemon Juice from Concentrate
⅓ cup orange juice
¼ cup vegetable oil
¼ cup whiskey
1 small onion, thinly sliced
12 peppercorns
1 teaspoon salt
1 medium orange, thinly sliced

Place steak in shallow baking dish. In small saucepan, combine remaining ingredients except orange. Over low heat, simmer 5 minutes; pour over meat. Top with orange slices; cover. Refrigerate 4 to 6 hours, turning occasionally. Remove meat from marinade; grill or broil as desired. Heat remaining marinade and serve with steak.

PEPPER & HERB MARINADE

Makes about ¾ cup

½ cup ReaLemon® Lemon Juice from Concentrate
⅓ cup vegetable oil
1 tablespoon instant minced onion
1 clove garlic, finely chopped
1 tablespoon sugar
2 teaspoons hot pepper sauce
2 teaspoons Wyler's® Beef-Flavor Instant Bouillon
1 teaspoon thyme leaves
¼ teaspoon oregano leaves

In small saucepan, combine ingredients; heat until bouillon dissolves. Cool. Pour over meat or poultry. Refrigerate 6 hours or overnight, turning occasionally. Remove meat from marinade; grill or broil as desired, basting frequently with marinade.

BEER MARINATED STEAK

Makes 4 to 6 servings

1 large onion, thinly sliced
2 cloves garlic, finely chopped
½ cup vegetable oil
1 cup beer
½ cup ReaLemon® Lemon Juice
  from Concentrate
2 tablespoons light brown sugar
1 tablespoon Worcestershire
  sauce
1 (1- to 1½-pound) flank steak,
  scored

In medium skillet, cook onion and
garlic in ¼ *cup* oil until tender; remove
from heat. Add remaining ingredients
except meat. Place meat in shallow
baking dish; pour marinade over.
Cover; refrigerate 6 hours or overnight,
turning occasionally. Remove meat
from marinade; grill or broil as desired,
basting frequently with marinade.

Beer Marinated Steak

BARBECUE MARINADE

Makes about 1 cup

½ cup prepared barbecue sauce
¼ cup vegetable oil
¼ cup ReaLemon® Lemon Juice
  from Concentrate
1 tablespoon brown sugar

In small bowl, combine ingredients.
Pour over meat or poultry. Refrigerate
6 hours or overnight, turning occasionally. Remove meat from marinade; grill
or broil as desired, basting frequently
with marinade.

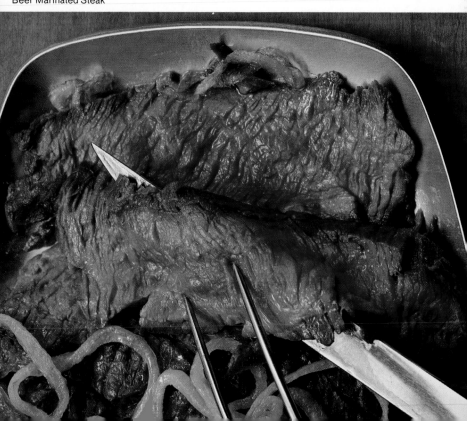

CURRIED TURKEY AND HAM CROISSANTS ▲

Makes 8 servings

1 (10-ounce) package frozen
asparagus spears or 1 pound
fresh asparagus, cooked and
drained
12 ounces thinly sliced ham
12 ounces thinly sliced turkey
6 ounces sliced Swiss cheese
8 croissants, split in half
Curry Sauce

Preheat oven to 350°. Arrange asparagus, equal amounts of ham, turkey
and cheese on bottom half of each
croissant. Place top halves of croissants
on cheese. Bake 10 to 15 minutes or
until hot. Meanwhile, make Curry Sauce;
spoon over croissants. Garnish with
paprika if desired. Refrigerate
leftovers.

Curry Sauce

¼ cup margarine or butter
2 tablespoons flour
½ teaspoon curry powder
¼ teaspoon salt
1½ cups coffee cream or milk
¼ cup ReaLemon® Lemon Juice
from Concentrate

In small saucepan, melt margarine; stir
in flour, curry and salt. Gradually add
cream; over medium heat, cook and stir
until thickened, about 5 minutes.
Remove from heat; slowly stir in
ReaLemon. (Makes about 1½ cups)

LEMONY GLAZED AND STUFFED CHICKEN

Makes 4 to 6 servings

1 (3- to 4-pound) whole broiler-
fryer chicken
Vegetable oil
Salt and pepper
¾ cup chopped celery
½ cup chopped onion
½ cup plus 1 tablespoon margarine or butter
1 cup plus 2 tablespoons water
2 teaspoons Wyler's® Chicken-
Flavor Instant Bouillon
1 (8-ounce) package herb-
seasoned stuffing mix
¼ cup ReaLemon® Lemon Juice
from Concentrate
1 small clove garlic, finely
chopped
1 teaspoon cornstarch

Preheat oven to 375°. Brush chicken
with oil; season with salt and pepper. In
large skillet, cook celery and onion in
½ cup margarine until tender; add 1
cup water and 1 teaspoon bouillon.
Cook until bouillon dissolves. Remove
from heat; stir in stuffing mix and 2
tablespoons ReaLemon. Stuff chicken
loosely; truss. Place breast-side up on
rack in shallow roasting pan. Bake 1
hour and 15 minutes. Turn remaining
stuffing into 1-quart baking dish.
Meanwhile, to make glaze, in small
saucepan, cook garlic in remaining
1 tablespoon margarine. Stir in remaining 2 tablespoons water and 1 teaspoon
bouillon. Stir cornstarch into remaining
2 tablespoons ReaLemon; add to
bouillon mixture. Over low heat, cook
and stir until thickened. Brush chicken
with glaze; return to oven along with
stuffing. Bake 15 minutes. Refrigerate
leftovers.

To Make Gravy: In drippings, add ¼ cup
flour; stir until smooth and well blended.
Add 2 cups water and 2 teaspoons
Wyler's® Chicken-Flavor Instant
Bouillon; cook and stir until thickened.

Continued next page

Lemony Glazed and Stuffed Chicken

MICROWAVE: Prepare chicken and stuffing as above. Place chicken breast-side down on rack in 12x7-inch baking dish; cover with wax paper. Microwave on full power (high) 15 minutes. Turn chicken breast-side up; cover with wax paper. Microwave on full power (high) 10 to 15 minutes or until tender. Meanwhile, prepare glaze as above. Brush chicken with glaze during last 5 minutes of cooking time. Turn remaining stuffing into 1-quart round baking dish; cover with plastic wrap. Microwave on full power (high) 2 to 3 minutes. Combine gravy ingredients as above. Microwave on full power (high) 7 to 8 minutes or until thickened, stirring occasionally.

PEPPER CHICKEN ▶

Makes 4 servings

- 1 (2½- to 3-pound) broiler-fryer chicken, cut up, breaded and fried
- 3 cups water
- ¼ cup firmly packed brown sugar
- ¼ cup ReaLemon® Lemon Juice from Concentrate from Concentrate
- 4 teaspoons Wyler's® Chicken-Flavor Instant Bouillon or 4 Chicken-Flavor Bouillon Cubes
- 2 tablespoons soy sauce
- 1½ teaspoons garlic powder
- 1½ teaspoons ground ginger
- 3 tablespoons cornstarch
- 2 medium green peppers, cut into strips
- 1 cup diagonally sliced celery
- 1 large onion, sliced

In medium saucepan, combine 2½ *cups* water, sugar, ReaLemon, bouillon, soy sauce, garlic powder and ginger; cook and stir until bouillon dissolves. Mix cornstarch with remaining ½ *cup* water; stir into bouillon mixture. Cook until thickened. In large skillet, arrange chicken and vegetables; pour sauce over. Cover; cook 15 minutes or until vegetables are tender crisp. Serve with rice. Refrigerate leftovers.

LEMON HERB CORNISH HENS

Makes 4 servings

2 (1½-pound) Rock Cornish
   hens, split in half lengthwise
Salt and pepper
2 tablespoons finely chopped
   onion
1 clove garlic, finely chopped
¼ cup vegetable oil
¼ cup ReaLemon® Lemon Juice
   from Concentrate
2 teaspoons Wyler's® Chicken-
   Flavor Instant Bouillon *or*
   2 Chicken-Flavor Bouillon
   Cubes
1 teaspoon chopped parsley
1 teaspoon rosemary leaves,
   crushed

Season hens lightly with salt and
pepper. In small saucepan, cook onion
and garlic in oil until tender. Add
remaining ingredients; simmer 10
minutes. Grill hens until tender and
crisp, about 1 hour, turning and basting
frequently with sauce. Refrigerate
leftovers.

Oven Method: Place hens on rack in
roasting pan. Bake at 375° for 1 hour
and 15 minutes, basting frequently.

Lemon Herb Cornish Hens

OVEN BARBECUED CHICKEN

Makes 4 to 6 servings

1 (2½- to 3-pound) broiler-fryer
   chicken, cut up
1 cup unsifted flour
1 teaspoon salt
6 tablespoons margarine or
   butter, melted
¼ cup chopped onion
1 clove garlic, finely chopped
1 cup catsup
¼ cup firmly packed light brown
   sugar
¼ cup ReaLemon® Lemon Juice
   from Concentrate
¼ cup water
2 tablespoons Worcestershire
   sauce

Preheat oven to 350°. In paper or
plastic bag, combine flour and salt. Add
chicken, a few pieces at a time; shake
to coat. Place in greased 13x9-inch
baking dish; drizzle with ¼ cup margarine. Bake 30 minutes. Meanwhile, in
small saucepan, cook onion and garlic
in remaining 2 tablespoons margarine
until tender. Add remaining ingredients; simmer uncovered 10 minutes.
Pour over chicken; bake 30 minutes
longer or until tender. Refrigerate
leftovers.

CRISP 'N' SALTY GRILLED CHICKEN ▶

Makes 4 to 6 servings

¼ cup margarine or butter
½ cup ReaLemon® Lemon Juice
    from Concentrate
½ cup water
4 teaspoons soy sauce
1 tablespoon salt
1 (2½- to 3-pound) broiler-fryer
    chicken, cut up

In small saucepan, melt margarine; stir in ReaLemon, water, soy sauce and salt. Grill or broil as desired, turning and basting frequently with sauce. Refrigerate leftovers.

TANGY LIME BROILED CHICKEN

Makes 4 to 6 servings

1 (2½- to 3-pound) broiler-fryer
    chicken, cut up
1 (8-ounce) bottle ReaLime®
    Lime Juice from Concentrate
¼ cup margarine or butter
2 teaspoons soy sauce

Place chicken in shallow baking dish; pour ReaLime over chicken. Cover; refrigerate 6 hours or overnight, turning chicken occasionally. Reserving ⅔ cup ReaLime, remove and drain chicken; place on broiler tray. In small saucepan, melt margarine; stir in reserved ReaLime and soy sauce. Grill or broil as desired, turning and basting frequently with sauce. Refrigerate leftovers.

SOUR CREAM CHICKEN & NOODLES

Makes 6 servings

3 whole chicken breasts, split
    (about 2½ pounds)
1 (16-ounce) container sour
    cream
1 tablespoon Worcestershire
    sauce
⅓ cup ReaLemon® Lemon Juice
    from Concentrate
2 teaspoons celery salt
¼ teaspoon garlic powder
¾ cup dry bread crumbs
¼ cup margarine or butter,
    melted
½ (1-pound) package Creamette®
    Medium Egg Noodles,
    cooked and drained
¼ cup chopped green onions or
    chives

In small bowl, combine sour cream, Worcestershire, ReaLemon, celery salt and garlic powder. In large bowl, layer chicken and sour cream mixture. Cover; refrigerate overnight. Preheat oven to 350°. Reserving sour cream sauce, coat chicken with crumbs. Arrange in greased 13x9-inch baking dish. Drizzle with margarine. Bake uncovered 45 to 50 minutes or until tender. Meanwhile, in large saucepan, over low heat, cook and stir reserved sauce until hot. Add noodles and onions; mix well. Heat through. Serve chicken with noodles. Refrigerate leftovers.

SESAME CHICKEN ORIENTAL

Makes 4 to 6 servings

1 (2½- to 3-pound) broiler-fryer chicken, cut up
¼ cup margarine or butter
1 (12-ounce) jar pineapple preserves or orange marmalade (1 cup)
¼ cup ReaLemon® Lemon Juice from Concentrate
1 tablespoon brown sugar
2 teaspoons cornstarch
2 teaspoons soy sauce
1 tablespoon sesame seeds, toasted
1 (11-ounce) can mandarin orange segments, drained
½ cup sliced water chestnuts

Preheat oven to 350°. In large skillet, brown chicken in margarine on all sides; arrange in greased 13x9-inch baking dish. In small saucepan, combine preserves, ReaLemon, sugar, cornstarch and soy sauce; bring to a boil. Pour over chicken. Sprinkle with sesame seeds. Bake uncovered 50 minutes, basting occasionally. Add orange segments and water chestnuts; baste. Continue baking 10 minutes or until chicken is tender. Garnish as desired. Refrigerate leftovers.

LEMON CHICKEN

Makes 4 servings

1¼ pounds boneless chicken breasts, skinned and cut into bite-size pieces
1 egg, slightly beaten
3 tablespoons cornstarch
2 tablespoons soy sauce
½ cup sugar
2 teaspoons Wyler's® Chicken-Flavor Instant Bouillon
½ teaspoon garlic powder
1 cup water
½ cup ReaLemon® Lemon Juice from Concentrate
2 tablespoons catsup
Vegetable oil
Additional cornstarch
Shredded lettuce or hot cooked rice

In medium bowl, combine egg, 1 tablespoon cornstarch and soy sauce; mix well. Add chicken, stirring to coat; marinate 10 minutes. Meanwhile, in medium saucepan, combine remaining 2 tablespoons cornstarch, sugar, bouillon and garlic powder. Gradually add water, ReaLemon and catsup; mix well. Over high heat, cook and stir until mixture comes to a boil. Reduce heat; continue cooking and stirring until mixture thickens. Keep sauce warm. Coat chicken with additional cornstarch. In large skillet, cook chicken in ½ inch hot oil until tender and golden. Arrange chicken on shredded lettuce; pour warm sauce over chicken. Garnish as desired. Serve immediately. Refrigerate leftovers.

Pictured: Sesame Chicken Oriental, Lemon Chicken.

BAKED APRICOT CHICKEN ▲

Makes 4 to 6 servings

1 (12-ounce) jar apricot or peach
  preserves (1 cup)
¼ cup ReaLemon® Lemon Juice
  from Concentrate
2 teaspoons soy sauce
½ teaspoon salt
1 (2½- to 3-pound) broiler-fryer
  chicken, cut up
1 cup dry bread crumbs
¼ cup margarine or butter,
  melted

Preheat oven to 350°. In shallow dish,
combine preserves, ReaLemon, soy
sauce and salt. Coat chicken with
apricot mixture; roll in bread crumbs.
Set aside remaining apricot mixture. In
greased 13x9-inch baking dish, arrange
chicken; drizzle with margarine. Bake
uncovered 1 hour or until tender. Heat
remaining apricot mixture; serve with
chicken. Refrigerate leftovers.

MARINATED GINGER CHICKEN

Makes 4 to 6 servings

1 (2½- to 3-pound) broiler-fryer
  chicken, cut up
½ cup ReaLemon® Lemon Juice
  from Concentrate
½ cup vegetable oil
¼ cup soy sauce
1 teaspoon grated ginger root *or*
  1 tablespoon ground ginger
1 teaspoon onion salt
¼ teaspoon garlic powder

Place chicken in shallow baking dish. In
small bowl, combine remaining ingredients; pour over chicken. Cover; refrigerate 4 hours or overnight, turning
occasionally. Grill or broil as desired,
basting frequently with marinade.
Refrigerate leftovers.

MICROWAVE: Prepare chicken as
above, marinating in 12x7-inch baking
dish. Cover with wax paper; microwave
in marinade on full power (high) 20 to
25 minutes or until tender, rearranging
pieces once.

ELEGANT CHICKEN PICCATA

Makes 4 servings

⅓ cup plus 1 tablespoon unsifted
    flour
½ teaspoon paprika
 4 boneless chicken breast
    halves, skinned
 3 tablespoons margarine or
    butter
¼ cup water
 2 cups (1 pint) coffee cream or
    half-and-half
 1 tablespoon Wyler's® Chicken-
    Flavor Instant Bouillon or
    3 Chicken-Flavor Bouillon
    Cubes
 2 tablespoons dry sherry
 2 tablespoons ReaLemon®
    Lemon Juice from
    Concentrate
½ to ¾ cup shredded Swiss
    cheese
   Hot cooked rice

Preheat oven to 350°. In paper or
plastic bag, combine ⅓ cup flour and
paprika. Add chicken, a few pieces at a
time; shake to coat. In large skillet, over
medium heat, brown chicken in margarine on both sides until golden
brown. Add water; cover and simmer 20
minutes. Remove chicken; arrange in
12x7-inch baking dish. Stir remaining
1 tablespoon flour into drippings.
Gradually add cream and bouillon.
Over low heat, cook and stir until
slightly thickened and bouillon is
dissolved, about 5 to 10 minutes. Add
sherry and ReaLemon; pour over
chicken. Bake covered 20 minutes.
Uncover; top with cheese. Continue
baking 5 minutes. Serve with rice.
Refrigerate leftovers.

SPECIAL LEMONY CHICKEN

Makes 6 servings

¼ cup unsifted flour
 1 teaspoon salt
¼ teaspoon pepper
 6 boneless chicken breast
    halves, skinned
¼ cup margarine or butter
¼ cup ReaLemon® Lemon Juice
    from Concentrate
 8 ounces fresh mushrooms,
    sliced (about 2 cups)
   Hot cooked rice
   Chopped parsley

In paper or plastic bag, combine flour,
salt and pepper. Add chicken, a few
pieces at a time; shake to coat. In large
skillet, brown chicken in margarine on
both sides until golden brown. Add
ReaLemon and mushrooms. Reduce
heat; cover and simmer 20 minutes or
until tender. Serve over rice; garnish
with parsley. Refrigerate leftovers.

Special Lemony Chicken

Vegetables

Asparagus to zucchini—vegetables of all kinds—perk up with a dash of ReaLemon. Serve a simple butter sauce or our easy but elegant Hollandaise for a winning way to enhance broccoli or green beans. For cauliflower, carrots or cabbage, cook in a glaze or sweet 'n' sour sauce.

SAVORY LEMON VEGETABLES

Makes 8 servings

6 slices bacon, cooked and crumbled, reserving ¼ cup drippings
1 pound carrots, pared and sliced
1 medium head cauliflower, core removed
1 cup finely chopped onion
½ cup ReaLemon® Lemon Juice from Concentrate
½ cup water
4 teaspoons sugar
1 teaspoon salt
1 teaspoon thyme leaves
Chopped parsley

In large saucepan, cook carrots and cauliflower in water until tender. Meanwhile, in medium skillet, cook onion in drippings. Add ReaLemon, water, sugar, salt and thyme; bring to a boil. Drain vegetables; arrange in serving dish. Pour warm sauce over vegetables. Garnish with bacon and parsley.

MICROWAVE: Microwave bacon, reserving ¼ *cup* drippings. On large glass platter with rim, arrange cauliflower and carrots. Cover with plastic wrap; microwave on full power (high) 14 to 16 minutes. In 1-quart bowl, microwave bacon drippings and onion on full power (high) 1 minute. Add ReaLemon, water, sugar, salt and thyme. Microwave on full power (high) 5½ to 6 minutes or until sauce boils. Proceed as above.

OVEN GERMAN POTATO SALAD

Makes 6 servings

1 pound potatoes, cooked,
    peeled and sliced (about 3
    cups)
6 slices bacon, cooked and
    crumbled, reserving 3
    tablespoons drippings
2 tablespoons chopped onion
¼ cup sugar
1 tablespoon cornstarch
½ teaspoon dry mustard
1 teaspoon salt
½ cup water
¼ cup ReaLemon® Lemon Juice
    from Concentrate
¼ cup cider vinegar
¼ cup chopped celery

In 2-quart shallow baking dish, combine potatoes, bacon and onion; set
aside. In small saucepan, combine
sugar, cornstarch, mustard and salt.
Gradually add reserved drippings,
water, ReaLemon and vinegar; mix
well. Over medium heat, cook and stir
until thickened; pour over potatoes. Let
stand several hours to blend flavors; stir
in celery. Bake at 350° for 30 minutes
or until hot.

Tip: Recipe can be doubled. Use 2½-
quart shallow baking dish.

RED CABBAGE 'N' APPLES ▲

Makes 6 to 8 servings

¼ cup margarine or butter
⅓ cup ReaLemon® Lemon Juice
    from Concentrate
¼ cup firmly packed light brown
    sugar
¼ cup water
½ teaspoon caraway seeds
½ teaspoon salt
4 cups shredded red cabbage
2 medium red all-purpose apples,
    cored and coarsely chopped

In large saucepan, melt margarine; stir
in ReaLemon, sugar, water, caraway
and salt. Add cabbage and apples;
bring to a boil. Reduce heat; cover and
simmer 25 to 30 minutes.

MICROWAVE: In 2-quart round baking
dish, microwave margarine on full
power (high) 45 seconds or until
melted. Stir in ReaLemon, sugar, water,
caraway and salt; add cabbage and
apples. Cover with plastic wrap; microwave on full power (high) 15 to 23
minutes, stirring every 5 minutes. Let
stand 2 minutes before serving.

LEMON ORANGE CARROTS

Makes 6 servings

3 cups pared, sliced carrots,
    cooked and drained
½ cup orange marmalade
2 tablespoons ReaLemon®
    Lemon Juice from
    Concentrate
2 tablespoons margarine or
    butter

In medium saucepan, combine carrots,
marmalade, ReaLemon and margarine;
stir to coat evenly. Heat through.

SKILLET ZUCCHINI AND MUSHROOMS

Makes 6 to 8 servings

4 cups sliced zucchini (about 1 pound)
1 cup sliced fresh mushrooms (about 4 ounces)
¼ cup chopped onion
¼ cup margarine or butter
3 tablespoons ReaLemon® Lemon Juice from Concentrate
¼ teaspoon Italian seasoning
¼ teaspoon salt

In large skillet, cook zucchini, mushrooms and onion in margarine until tender-crisp. Add remaining ingredients; heat through.

CITRUS CANDIED SWEET POTATOES

Makes 6 to 8 servings

2 (17- or 18-ounce) cans sweet potatoes, drained
1¼ cups firmly packed light brown sugar
2 tablespoons cornstarch
¾ cup orange juice
¼ cup ReaLemon® Lemon Juice from Concentrate
2 tablespoons margarine or butter, melted

Preheat oven to 350°. In 2-quart shallow baking dish, arrange sweet potatoes. In medium bowl, combine sugar and cornstarch; add orange juice, ReaLemon and margarine. Pour over sweet potatoes. Bake 50 to 55 minutes, basting occasionally with sauce.

MICROWAVE: Arrange sweet potatoes as above. In 1-quart glass measure, combine sugar and cornstarch. Add orange juice, ReaLemon and margarine. Microwave on full power (high) 5 to 6 minutes until slightly thickened, stirring every 2 minutes. Pour glaze over sweet potatoes; microwave on full power (high) 8 minutes, basting with glaze after 4 minutes. Let stand 2 minutes before serving.

LEMON PARSLIED POTATOES

Makes 6 to 8 servings

⅓ cup margarine or butter
¼ cup ReaLemon® Lemon Juice from Concentrate
1 tablespoon Wyler's® Chicken-Flavor Instant Bouillon or 3 Chicken-Flavor Bouillon Cubes
½ teaspoon hot pepper sauce, optional
1 tablespoon chopped parsley or chives
2 pounds small new potatoes, cooked

In small saucepan, melt margarine; add remaining ingredients except potatoes. Heat until bouillon dissolves; pour over hot potatoes, stirring to coat.

MICROWAVE: In 2-cup glass measure, microwave margarine on full power (high) 30 seconds or until melted. Add remaining ingredients except potatoes. Microwave on full power (high) 1½ to 2 minutes or until bouillon is dissolved, stirring after first minute. Proceed as above.

Citrus Candied Sweet Potatoes

BLENDER HOLLANDAISE SAUCE

Makes about ¾ cup

2 egg yolks*
**1 to 2 tablespoons ReaLemon®
   Lemon Juice from
   Concentrate**
Dash cayenne pepper
½ cup butter or margarine, melted

In blender container, blend egg yolks, ReaLemon and pepper. Turn blender to high; *slowly* pour in butter, blending until thick, about 30 seconds. To serve, slowly heat in top of double boiler over hot water. Do not overheat. Refrigerate leftovers.

Tip: Recipe can be doubled.

MICROWAVE: To reheat sauce, pour into 1-cup glass measure. Microwave on ⅓ power (low) 2 minutes, stirring every 30 seconds.

*Use only Grade A clean, uncracked eggs.

VERSATILE VEGETABLE TOPPING

Makes about 1½ cups

**1 (3-ounce) package cream
   cheese, softened**
1 (8-ounce) container sour cream
**2 tablespoons ReaLemon®
   Lemon Juice from
   Concentrate**
**2 teaspoons prepared
   horseradish**
**1 teaspoon parsley flakes or
   chives**
**1 teaspoon Wyler's® Chicken-
   Flavor Instant Bouillon**
⅛ teaspoon pepper

In small mixer bowl, beat cheese until fluffy. Add remaining ingredients; mix well. Chill 2 to 3 hours to blend flavors. Stir before serving. Serve on baked potatoes, cooked vegetables or as a dip for chips or raw vegetables. Refrigerate leftovers.

LEMONY CREAM SAUCE

Makes about 1½ cups

**¼ cup ReaLemon® Lemon Juice
   from Concentrate**
2 egg yolks
¼ cup margarine or butter
**1 to 2 teaspoons Wyler's®
   Chicken-Flavor Instant
   Bouillon *or* 2 Chicken-Flavor
   Bouillon Cubes**
Dash cayenne pepper
**1 (8-ounce) container sour
   cream, at room temperature**

In small saucepan, combine ReaLemon and egg yolks; add margarine, bouillon and pepper. Over low heat, cook and stir until thickened and bouillon dissolves. Slowly stir in sour cream; heat through. Serve with assorted cooked vegetables. Refrigerate leftovers.

Tip: Sauce can be chilled to use as dip for raw vegetables.

MICROWAVE: In 1-quart glass measure, microwave margarine on full power (high) 30 seconds or until melted. Stir in ReaLemon and egg yolks; mix well. Add bouillon and pepper. Microwave on ⅔ power (medium-high) 2 to 2½ minutes until thick, stirring every 30 seconds. Proceed as above.

ALMONDINE BUTTER SAUCE

Makes ⅔ cup

½ cup sliced almonds
⅓ cup margarine or butter
**¼ cup ReaLemon® Lemon Juice
   from Concentrate**

In small skillet, over medium low heat, cook almonds in margarine until golden; remove from heat. Stir in ReaLemon. Serve warm over cooked vegetables or fish.

Breads, Cakes & Cookies

The wonderful cinnamon-scented aromas wafting from the oven promise warm muffins, gooey pecan sticky buns, luscious lemon cakes, cookies— crisp or chewy, and moist quick bread loaves—as well as compliments to the cook!

LEMON BREAD

Makes one 9x5-inch loaf

2 cups unsifted flour
1 teaspoon baking powder
½ teaspoon baking soda
¼ teaspoon salt
1¼ cups sugar
½ cup margarine or butter, softened
3 eggs
½ cup ReaLemon® Lemon Juice from Concentrate
½ cup milk
¾ cup chopped pecans, optional
Clear Lemon Glaze*

Preheat oven to 350°. Stir together flour, baking powder, baking soda and salt; set aside. In large mixer bowl, beat sugar and margarine until fluffy. Add eggs, 1 at a time; beat well. Gradually beat in ReaLemon. Add milk alternately with dry ingredients; stir well. Add pecans if desired. Turn into greased and floured 9x5-inch loaf pan. Bake 50 to 55 minutes or until wooden pick inserted near center comes out clean. Remove from oven; drizzle with Lemon Glaze. Cool 15 minutes; remove from pan. Cool completely. Store tightly wrapped.

***Clear Lemon Glaze:** In small saucepan, combine 2 tablespoons sugar and 2 teaspoons ReaLemon; heat until sugar dissolves.

Pictured: Lemon Bread, Easy Lemon Glazed Cake (recipe page 86), Coconut Lemon Bars (recipe page 96).

EASY LEMON GLAZED CAKE

Makes one 10-inch cake

1 (18¼-ounce) package yellow
  cake mix
⅓ cup confectioners' sugar
¼ cup ReaLemon® Lemon Juice
  from Concentrate

Preheat oven to 350°. Prepare cake
mix according to package directions.
Pour into greased and floured 10-inch
bundt pan; bake 40 minutes or until
wooden pick inserted near center
comes out clean. While in pan, poke
holes in cake 1 inch apart. In small
bowl, combine sugar and ReaLemon;
slowly pour half the mixture over warm
cake. Let stand 10 minutes. Remove
from pan; pour remaining ReaLemon
mixture over cake. Cool. Sprinkle with
confectioners' sugar if desired.

LEMON PECAN STICKY ROLLS

Makes 16 rolls

½ cup granulated sugar
½ cup firmly packed light brown
  sugar
¼ cup margarine or butter
¼ cup ReaLemon® Lemon Juice
  from Concentrate
½ teaspoon ground cinnamon
½ cup chopped pecans
2 (8-ounce) packages refrigerated crescent rolls

Preheat oven to 375°. In small saucepan, combine sugars, margarine,
ReaLemon and cinnamon. Bring to a
boil; boil 1 minute. Reserving ¼ cup,
pour remaining ReaLemon mixture into
9-inch round layer cake pan. Sprinkle
with nuts. Separate rolls into 8 rec-
tangles; spread with reserved
ReaLemon mixture. Roll up jellyroll-
fashion, beginning with short side; seal
edges. Cut in half. Place rolls, cut-side
down, in prepared pan. Bake 30 to 35
minutes or until dark golden brown.
Loosen sides. Immediately turn onto
serving plate; do not remove pan. Let
stand 5 minutes; remove pan. Serve
warm.

Lemon Pecan Sticky Rolls

OLD-FASHIONED LEMON PUDDING CAKE ▲

Makes 6 to 8 servings

3 eggs, separated
1 cup sugar
¼ cup unsifted flour
¼ teaspoon salt
1 cup milk
¼ cup ReaLemon® Lemon Juice from Concentrate

Preheat oven to 325°. In small mixer bowl, beat egg whites until stiff but not dry; set aside. In medium bowl, combine sugar, flour and salt. In small bowl, beat egg yolks; stir in milk and ReaLemon. Add to flour mixture; mix well. Fold in egg whites; pour into 1-quart baking dish. Place in larger pan; fill with 1 inch hot water. Bake 50 to 55 minutes or until top is well-browned. Cool about 30 minutes before serving. Spoon pudding over cake in serving dishes. Refrigerate leftovers.

Individual Servings: Pour mixture into 8 (6-ounce) custard cups; place in shallow pan. Fill with 1 inch hot water. Bake 35 to 40 minutes.

CHERRY 'N' APPLE DUMP CAKE ▲

Makes one 9-inch cake

1 (21-ounce) can cherry pie filling
2 cups diced all-purpose apples (2 medium apples)
⅓ cup ReaLemon® Lemon Juice from Concentrate
½ cup cold margarine or butter
1 (9-ounce) package one-layer yellow cake mix
¾ cup chopped pecans

Preheat oven to 350°. In 9-inch square baking pan, combine pie filling, apples and ReaLemon. In medium bowl, cut margarine into cake mix until crumbly; add pecans. Sprinkle evenly over pie filling. Bake 40 to 45 minutes or until golden brown. Serve warm.

MICROWAVE: In 2-quart round baking dish, prepare as above. Microwave on full power (high) 12 to 14 minutes.

GOLDEN RAISIN SPICE BREAD

Makes one 9x5-inch loaf

2 cups unsifted flour
2 teaspoons baking powder
1 teaspoon ground cinnamon
½ teaspoon ground nutmeg
½ teaspoon salt
1 cup sugar
½ cup margarine or butter, softened
3 eggs
½ cup milk
½ cup ReaLemon® Lemon Juice from Concentrate
1 cup golden seedless raisins

Preheat oven to 350°. Stir together flour, baking powder, cinnamon, nutmeg and salt; set aside. In large mixer bowl, beat sugar and margarine until fluffy. Add eggs, 1 at a time; beat well. Add milk alternately with dry ingredients; stir well. Stir in ReaLemon and raisins. Turn into greased and floured 9x5-inch loaf pan. Bake 55 to 60 minutes or until wooden pick inserted near center comes out clean. Cool 10 minutes; remove from pan. Cool completely. Store tightly wrapped.

CREAM CHEESE SWIRL COFFEE CAKE ▶

Makes one 10-inch cake

2 (3-ounce) packages cream cheese, softened
2 tablespoons confectioners' sugar
2 tablespoons ReaLemon® Lemon Juice from Concentrate
2 cups unsifted flour
1 teaspoon baking powder
1 teaspoon baking soda
¼ teaspoon salt
1 cup granulated sugar
½ cup margarine or butter, softened
3 eggs
1 teaspoon vanilla extract
1 (8-ounce) container sour cream
Cinnamon-Nut Topping*

Preheat oven to 350°. In small bowl, beat cheese, confectioners' sugar and ReaLemon until smooth; set aside. Stir together flour, baking powder, baking soda and salt; set aside. In large mixer bowl, beat granulated sugar and margarine until fluffy. Add eggs and vanilla; mix well. Add dry ingredients alternately with sour cream; mix well. Pour half of batter into greased and floured 10-inch tube pan. Spoon cheese mixture on top of batter to within ½ inch of pan edge. Spoon remaining batter over filling, spreading to pan edge. Sprinkle with Cinnamon Nut Topping. Bake 40 to 45 minutes or until wooden pick inserted near center comes out clean. Cool 10 minutes; remove from pan. Serve warm.

*Cinnamon-Nut Topping: Combine ¼ cup finely chopped nuts, 2 tablespoons granulated sugar and ½ teaspoon ground cinnamon.

LEMON TEA MUFFINS ▲

Makes about 1½ dozen

2 cups unsifted flour
2 teaspoons baking powder
½ teaspoon salt
1 cup margarine or butter,
softened
1 cup granulated sugar
4 eggs, separated
½ cup ReaLemon® Lemon Juice
from Concentrate
¼ cup finely chopped nuts
2 tablespoons light brown sugar
¼ teaspoon ground nutmeg

Preheat oven to 375°. Stir together
flour, baking powder and salt; set aside.
In large mixer bowl, beat margarine and
granulated sugar until fluffy. Add egg
yolks; beat until light. Gradually stir in
ReaLemon alternately with dry ingredients *(do not overmix)*. In small mixer
bowl, beat egg whites until stiff but not
dry; fold one-third egg whites into
ReaLemon mixture. Fold remaining
egg whites into ReaLemon mixture. Fill
paper-lined or greased muffin cups ¾
full. Combine remaining ingredients;
sprinkle evenly over muffins. Bake 15
to 20 minutes. Cool 5 minutes; remove
from pan. Serve warm.

LEMON BUTTER FROSTING

Makes 2¼ cups, enough to frost one
2-layer cake or 36 cupcakes

½ cup margarine or butter,
softened
1 pound confectioners' sugar
(about 4 cups)
¼ cup ReaLemon® Lemon Juice
from Concentrate

In small mixer bowl, beat margarine
and *1 cup* sugar until light and fluffy.
Gradually add ReaLemon alternately
with remaining *3 cups* sugar, beating
until light and fluffy.

LEMON CREAM CHEESE
FROSTING

Makes about 1½ cups

1 (3-ounce) package cream
cheese, softened
2 tablespoons margarine or
butter, softened
3 cups unsifted confectioners'
sugar
2 tablespoons ReaLemon®
Lemon Juice from
Concentrate

In small mixer bowl, beat cheese
and margarine until light and fluffy.
Gradually add sugar alternately with
ReaLemon. Chill 1 hour or until of
spreading consistency.

GINGERBREAD LEMON CAKE ROLL

Makes one 10-inch cake roll

¾ **cup unsifted flour**
¾ **teaspoon ground cinnamon**
¾ **teaspoon ground ginger**
½ **teaspoon baking powder**
½ **teaspoon baking soda**
¼ **teaspoon ground allspice**
¼ **teaspoon ground cloves**
4 **eggs**
½ **cup sugar**
⅓ **cup light molasses**
 Confectioners' sugar
 Lemon Cheese Filling

Preheat oven to 375°. Stir together flour, spices, baking powder and baking soda; set aside. In large mixer bowl, beat eggs until thick and lemon-colored; gradually add sugar, beating until very thick. Add molasses; mix well. Stir in dry ingredients. Grease 15x10-inch jellyroll pan; line with wax paper and grease again. Pour batter into prepared pan. Bake 10 to 12 minutes or until cake springs back when lightly touched. Immediately loosen sides; turn onto towel sprinkled with confectioners' sugar. Remove wax paper. Starting at narrow end, roll cake with towel; cool thoroughly. Unroll; spread with chilled Lemon Cheese Filling. Roll up; chill. Sprinkle with confectioners' sugar before serving.

Lemon Cheese Filling

¾ **cup sugar**
2 **tablespoons cornstarch**
⅔ **cup water**
2 **egg yolks, beaten**
¼ **cup ReaLemon® Lemon Juice from Concentrate**
1 **(3-ounce) package cream cheese, softened**
2 **tablespoons margarine or butter, softened**

In medium saucepan, combine sugar and cornstarch. Gradually add water, egg yolks and ReaLemon; mix well. Over medium heat, cook and stir until mixture thickens and boils; remove from heat. Add cheese and margarine; beat until smooth. Chill, stirring occasionally. (Makes about 1⅔ cups)

LEMON WALNUT COFFEE CAKE

Makes one 8-inch cake

1 **cup firmly packed light brown sugar**
2 **tablespoons flour**
1 **teaspoon ground cinnamon**
5 **tablespoons margarine or butter, melted**
1 **cup chopped walnuts**
2 **cups biscuit baking mix**
1 **egg, beaten**
¼ **cup milk**
2 **tablespoons ReaLemon® Lemon Juice from Concentrate**
 Lemon Glaze*

Preheat oven to 400°. To make topping, in small bowl, stir together ½ cup sugar, flour, cinnamon and 2 tablespoons margarine until crumbly. Add ½ cup nuts; set aside. In medium bowl, combine biscuit mix, remaining ½ cup sugar and remaining ½ cup nuts. Add egg, milk, remaining 3 tablespoons margarine and ReaLemon; mix until moistened. Turn into greased 8-inch square baking pan; sprinkle with topping. Bake 25 minutes or until wooden pick inserted near center comes out clean. Cool 15 minutes; drizzle with Lemon Glaze.

***Lemon Glaze:** In small bowl, combine ⅓ cup confectioners' sugar and 2 to 3 teaspoons ReaLemon.

Gingerbread Cake Roll

STRAWBERRIES & CREAM ANGEL CAKE

Makes one 10-inch cake

1 (10-inch) **prepared angel food cake**

2 (3-ounce) **packages cream cheese, softened**

1 (14-ounce) **can Eagle® Brand Sweetened Condensed Milk (NOT evaporated milk)**

⅓ cup **ReaLemon® Lemon Juice from Concentrate**

1 teaspoon **almond extract**

2 to 3 drops **red food coloring, optional**

1 cup (½ pint) **whipping cream, whipped**

1 cup **chopped fresh strawberries Additional fresh strawberries, optional**

Cut 1-inch slice crosswise from top of cake; set aside. With sharp knife, cut around cake 1 inch from center hole and 1 inch from outer edge, leaving cake walls 1 inch thick. Remove cake from center, leaving 1-inch thick base on bottom of cake. Reserve cake pieces. In large mixer bowl, beat cheese until fluffy. Gradually add sweetened condensed milk; beat until smooth. Stir in ReaLemon, extract and food coloring if desired; mix well. Fold in whipped cream. Reserve two-thirds of mixture; refrigerate. Fold strawberries and reserved torn cake pieces except top into remaining one-third of mixture; fill cake cavity. Replace top slice of cake; frost with reserved whipped cream mixture. Chill 3 hours or until set. Garnish cake with additional strawberries if desired. Store in refrigerator.

LEMON CARROT CAKE SUPREME ▶

Makes one 10-inch cake

- 1 (9-ounce) package None Such® Condensed Mincemeat, crumbled
- 2 cups finely shredded carrots
- ½ cup chopped nuts
- 2 cups unsifted flour
- 1 cup firmly packed light brown sugar
- ¾ cup vegetable oil
- ¼ cup ReaLemon® Lemon Juice from Concentrate
- 3 eggs
- 2 teaspoons baking powder
- 1 teaspoon baking soda
- 1 teaspoon salt
  Cream Cheese Fluff
  Golden Lemon Sauce

Preheat oven to 325°. In large bowl, combine mincemeat, carrots and nuts; toss with ½ cup flour. Set aside. In large mixer bowl, combine sugar, oil and ReaLemon; beat well. Add eggs, 1 at a time, beating well after each addition. Stir together remaining 1½ cups flour, baking powder, baking soda and salt; gradually add to batter, beating until smooth. Stir in mincemeat mixture; mix well. Turn into well-greased and floured 10-inch bundt or tube pan. Bake 1 hour or until wooden pick inserted near center comes out clean. Cool 15 minutes; turn out of pan. Serve with Cream Cheese Fluff and warm Golden Lemon Sauce.

Cream Cheese Fluff

- 1 (8-ounce) package cream cheese, softened
- 2 tablespoons confectioners' sugar
- 2 tablespoons milk

In small mixer bowl, beat ingredients until fluffy. Refrigerate leftovers. (Makes about 1 cup)

Golden Lemon Sauce

- 1 cup sugar
- 2 tablespoons cornstarch
- ½ cup ReaLemon® Lemon Juice from Concentrate
- ½ cup water
- ¼ cup margarine or butter
- 1 drop yellow food coloring, optional

In small saucepan, combine sugar and cornstarch; stir in ReaLemon and water. Over medium heat, cook and stir until mixture comes to a boil. Reduce heat; continue cooking and stirring 3 to 4 minutes or until thick and clear. Remove from heat. Stir in margarine and food coloring if desired. Serve warm. Refrigerate leftovers. (Makes about 1½ cups)

LEMON ICING

Makes about ½ cup

- 2 tablespoons margarine or butter
- 3 to 4 teaspoons ReaLemon® Lemon Juice from Concentrate
- 1 cup confectioners' sugar

In small saucepan, melt margarine with ReaLemon; remove from heat. Stir in sugar; mix well. Drizzle warm icing over 10-inch bundt or tube cake, coffee cake or sweet rolls.

93

LEMON BLOSSOM COOKIES

Makes about 6 dozen

**2 cups margarine or butter,
softened
1½ cups confectioners' sugar
¼ cup ReaLemon® Lemon Juice
from Concentrate
4 cups unsifted flour
Finely chopped nuts, optional
Assorted fruit preserves and
jams or pecan halves**

Preheat oven to 350°. In large mixer
bowl, beat margarine and sugar until
fluffy. Add ReaLemon; beat well.
Gradually add flour; mix well. Chill 2
hours. Shape into 1-inch balls; roll in
nuts if desired. Place 1 inch apart on
greased baking sheets. Press thumb in
center of each ball; fill with preserves
or pecan. Bake 14 to 16 minutes or until
lightly browned.

LEMON ICED
AMBROSIA BARS

Makes 36 bars

**1½ cups unsifted flour
⅓ cup confectioners' sugar
¾ cup cold margarine or butter
2 cups firmly packed light brown
sugar
4 eggs, beaten
1 cup flaked coconut
1 cup finely chopped pecans
3 tablespoons flour
½ teaspoon baking powder
Lemon Icing***

Preheat oven to 350°. In medium bowl,
combine flour and confectioners' sugar;
cut in margarine until crumbly. Press
onto bottom of lightly greased 13x9-
inch baking pan; bake 15 minutes.
Meanwhile, in large bowl, combine
remaining ingredients except icing; mix
well. Spread evenly over baked crust;
bake 20 to 25 minutes. Cool. Spread
with Lemon Icing; chill. Cut into bars.
Store covered in refrigerator.

*Lemon Icing: Mix 2 cups confectioners'
sugar, 3 tablespoons ReaLemon and 2
tablespoons softened margarine until
smooth. (Makes about ⅔ cup)

HOLIDAY CITRUS LOGS

Makes two 10-inch logs

1 (12-ounce) package vanilla
wafers, crushed (about 3
cups)
1 (8-ounce) package candied
cherries, coarsely chopped
1 (8-ounce) package chopped
dates (1¾ cups)
1 cup chopped pecans or
almonds
¼ cup ReaLemon® Lemon Juice
from Concentrate
2 tablespoons orange-flavored
liqueur
1 tablespoon white corn syrup
Additional white corn syrup,
heated
Additional finely chopped
pecans or sliced almonds,
toasted

In large bowl, combine all ingredients
except additional corn syrup and nuts.
Shape into two 10-inch logs. Brush with
corn syrup; roll in nuts. Wrap tightly;
refrigerate 3 to 4 days to blend flavors.
To serve, cut into ¼-inch slices.

SLICE 'N' BAKE LEMON COOKIES

Makes about 5 dozen

2¼ cups unsifted flour
¼ teaspoon baking soda
½ cup margarine or butter,
softened
½ cup shortening
½ cup granulated sugar
½ cup firmly packed light brown
sugar
1 egg
3 tablespoons ReaLemon®
Lemon Juice from
Concentrate
Egg white, beaten
Sliced almonds

Stir together flour and baking soda; set
aside. In large mixer bowl, beat margarine, shortening and sugars until
fluffy. Add egg; mix well. Gradually add
dry ingredients and ReaLemon; mix
well. Chill 2 hours; form into two 10-
inch rolls. Wrap well; freeze until firm.
Preheat oven to 350°. Cut rolls into
¼-inch slices; place 1 inch apart on
greased baking sheets. Brush with egg
white; top with almonds. Bake 10 to 12
minutes or until lightly browned.

Lemony Spritz Sticks

*Chocolate Glaze: In small saucepan, melt 3 ounces sweet cooking chocolate and 2 tablespoons margarine or butter. (Makes about ⅓ cup)

Tip: When using electric cookie gun, use decorator tip. Press dough onto greased baking sheets into ½x3-inch strips. Bake 8 to 10 minutes or until lightly browned on ends.

RICH LEMON BARS

Makes 30 bars

1½ cups plus 3 tablespoons
    unsifted flour
½ cup confectioners' sugar
¾ cup cold margarine or butter
4 eggs, slightly beaten
1½ cups granulated sugar
1 teaspoon baking powder
½ cup ReaLemon® Lemon Juice
    from Concentrate
Additional confectioners' sugar

Preheat oven to 350°. In medium bowl, combine *1½ cups* flour and confectioners' sugar; cut in margarine until crumbly. Press onto bottom of lightly greased 13x9-inch baking pan; bake 15 minutes. Meanwhile, in large bowl, combine remaining ingredients except confectioners' sugar; mix well. Pour over baked crust; bake 20 to 25 minutes or until golden brown. Cool. Cut into bars. Sprinkle with additional confectioners' sugar. Store covered in refrigerator; serve at room temperature.

Lemon Pecan Bars: Omit 3 tablespoons flour in lemon mixture. Sprinkle ¾ cup finely chopped pecans over top of lemon mixture. Bake as above.

Coconut Lemon Bars: Omit 3 tablespoons flour in lemon mixture. Sprinkle ¾ cup flaked coconut over top of lemon mixture. Bake as above.

LEMONY SPRITZ STICKS ▲

Makes about 8½ dozen

1 cup butter or margarine,
    softened
1 cup confectioners' sugar
¼ cup ReaLemon® Lemon Juice
    from Concentrate
2½ cups unsifted flour
¼ teaspoon salt
Chocolate Glaze*
Finely chopped nuts

Preheat oven to 375°. In large mixer bowl, beat butter and sugar until fluffy. Add ReaLemon; beat well. Stir in flour and salt; mix well. Place dough in cookie press with star-shaped plate. Press dough onto greased baking sheets into 3-inch strips. Bake 5 to 6 minutes or until lightly browned on ends. Cool 1 to 2 minutes; remove from baking sheets. Cool completely. Dip ends of cookies in Chocolate Glaze then into nuts.

Continued next column

LEMON SUGAR COOKIES

Makes about 8 dozen

3 cups unsifted flour
2 teaspoons baking powder
½ teaspoon salt
2 cups sugar
1 cup shortening
2 eggs
**¼ cup ReaLemon® Lemon Juice
    from Concentrate**
Additional sugar

Preheat oven to 350°. Stir together flour, baking powder and salt; set aside. In large mixer bowl, beat sugar and shortening until fluffy. Stir in dry ingredients, then ReaLemon; mix well. Chill 2 hours. Shape into 1¼-inch balls; roll in additional sugar. Place 2 inches apart on greased baking sheets; flatten. Bake 8 to 10 minutes or until lightly browned.

CHEESECAKE BARS

Makes 40 bars

2 cups unsifted flour
**1½ cups firmly packed brown
    sugar**
1 cup cold margarine or butter
1½ cups quick-cooking oats
**2 (8-ounce) packages cream
    cheese, softened**
½ cup granulated sugar
3 eggs
¼ cup milk
1 teaspoon vanilla extract
**¼ cup ReaLemon® Lemon Juice
    from Concentrate**

Preheat oven to 350°. In bowl, combine flour and brown sugar; cut in margarine until crumbly. Stir in oats. Reserving *1½ cups* mixture, press remainder into 15x10-inch jellyroll pan; bake 10 minutes. Meanwhile, in large mixer bowl, beat cheese and granulated sugar until fluffy. Add eggs; beat well. Add milk and vanilla, then ReaLemon; beat well. Pour over crust; sprinkle with reserved mixture. Bake 25 minutes or until lightly browned. Cool. Refrigerate.

LEMON CUT-OUT COOKIES

Makes about 4 to 5 dozen

2¾ cups unsifted flour
1 teaspoon baking powder
½ teaspoon baking soda
¼ teaspoon salt
**½ cup margarine or butter,
    softened**
1½ cups sugar
1 egg
**⅓ cup ReaLemon® Lemon Juice
    from Concentrate**
Lemon Icing*, optional

Stir together flour, baking powder, baking soda and salt; set aside. In large mixer bowl, beat margarine and sugar until fluffy; beat in egg. Gradually add dry ingredients alternately with ReaLemon; mix well (dough will be soft). Chill overnight in refrigerator or 2 hours in freezer. Preheat oven to 375°. On well-floured surface, roll out one-third of dough to ⅛-inch thickness; cut with floured cookie cutters. Place 1 inch apart on greased baking sheets; bake 8 to 10 minutes. Cool. Ice and decorate if desired.

***Lemon Icing:** Mix 1¼ cups confectioners' sugar and 2 tablespoons ReaLemon until smooth. Add food coloring if desired. (Makes about ½ cup)

Lemon Cut-Out Cookies

Pies

Glorious pies! From traditional ReaLemon Meringue to warm Deep Dish Peach, here's a potpourri of delicious pies. Choose easy Cherry Cheese for a quick finale. Create a sensation with Upside-Down Apple Walnut or spirited Margarita Pie.

REALEMON MERINGUE PIE

Makes one 9-inch pie

1 (9-inch) baked pastry shell
1⅔ cups sugar
6 tablespoons cornstarch
½ cup ReaLemon® Lemon Juice from Concentrate
1½ cups boiling water
4 eggs, separated*
2 tablespoons margarine or butter
¼ teaspoon cream of tartar
Mint leaves, optional

Preheat oven to 350°. In heavy saucepan, combine *1⅓ cups* sugar and cornstarch; add ReaLemon. In small bowl, beat egg yolks; add to ReaLemon mixture. Gradually add water, stirring constantly. Over medium heat, cook and stir until mixture boils and thickens, about 8 to 10 minutes. Remove from heat. Add margarine; stir until melted. Pour into prepared pastry shell. In small mixer bowl, beat egg whites with cream of tartar until soft peaks form; gradually add remaining *⅓ cup* sugar, beating until stiff but not dry. Spread on top of pie, sealing carefully to edge of shell. Bake 12 to 15 minutes or until golden brown. Cool. Chill before serving. Garnish with mint if desired. Refrigerate leftovers.

*Use only Grade A clean, uncracked eggs.

FLUFFY LEMON CHEESE PIE

Makes one 9-inch pie

- 1 (9-inch) baked pastry shell
- 2 eggs, separated*
- 1¼ cups sugar
- ⅓ cup cornstarch
- 1 cup hot water
- ⅓ cup ReaLemon® Lemon Juice from Concentrate
- 1 (3-ounce) package cream cheese, softened
- Raspberry Glaze*

In small bowl, beat egg yolks. In medium saucepan, combine *1 cup* sugar and cornstarch; add water, ReaLemon and egg yolks. Over low heat, cook and stir until thickened. Remove from heat. Add cheese; mix well. Cool. In small mixer bowl, beat egg whites until soft peaks form; gradually add remaining ¼ *cup* sugar, beating until stiff but not dry. Fold into lemon mixture; pour into prepared pastry shell. Chill 4 hours or until set. Serve with Raspberry Glaze. Refrigerate leftovers.

*Use only Grade A clean, uncracked eggs.

Continued next column

Fluffy Lemon Cheese Pie

Fluffy Lemon Cheese Pie

*Raspberry Glaze: Reserving syrup, drain 1 (10-ounce) package thawed frozen red raspberries. In small saucepan, combine syrup and 4 teaspoons cornstarch. Cook and stir until thickened and clear. Cool. Stir in raspberries.

UNBELIEVABLE LEMON PIE

Makes one 10-inch pie

- 1 (14-ounce) can Eagle® Brand Sweetened Condensed Milk (NOT evaporated milk)
- 1 cup water
- ½ cup ReaLemon® Lemon Juice from Concentrate
- ½ cup biscuit baking mix
- 3 eggs
- ¼ cup margarine or butter, softened
- 1½ teaspoons vanilla extract
- 1 cup flaked coconut

Preheat oven to 350°. In blender container, combine all ingredients except coconut. On low speed, blend 3 minutes. Pour into greased *10-inch* pie plate; let stand 5 minutes. Sprinkle with coconut. Bake 35 to 40 minutes or until knife inserted near edge comes out clean. Cool slightly; serve warm or cool. Refrigerate leftovers.

Fluffy Lemon Cheese Pie

KEY LIME PIE ▲

Makes one 8- or 9-inch pie

1 (8- or 9-inch) baked pastry shell
3 eggs, separated*
1 (14-ounce) can Eagle® Brand
   Sweetened Condensed Milk
   (NOT evaporated milk)
½ cup ReaLime® Lime Juice from
   Concentrate
   Few drops green food coloring,
   optional
¼ teaspoon cream of tartar
⅓ cup sugar

Preheat oven to 350°. In medium bowl, beat egg yolks; stir in sweetened condensed milk, ReaLime and food coloring. Pour into prepared pastry shell. In small mixer bowl, beat egg whites with cream of tartar until soft peaks form; gradually add sugar, beating until stiff but not dry. Spread on top of pie, sealing carefully to edge of shell. Bake 12 to 15 minutes or until golden brown. Cool. Chill before serving. Refrigerate leftovers.

Tip: For a lighter filling, fold 1 stiffly beaten egg white into filling mixture. Proceed as directed.

*Use only Grade A clean, uncracked eggs.

CREAMY LEMON MERINGUE PIE

Makes one 8- or 9-inch pie

1 (8- or 9-inch) baked pastry shell
   or 1 graham cracker crumb
   crust
3 eggs, separated*
1 (14-ounce) can Eagle® Brand
   Sweetened Condensed Milk
   (NOT evaporated milk)
½ cup ReaLemon® Lemon Juice
   from Concentrate
   Few drops yellow food coloring, optional
¼ teaspoon cream of tartar
⅓ cup sugar

Preheat oven to 350°. In medium bowl, beat egg yolks; stir in sweetened condensed milk, ReaLemon and food coloring. Pour into prepared pastry shell. In small mixer bowl, beat egg whites with cream of tartar until soft peaks form; gradually add sugar, beating until stiff but not dry. Spread on top of pie, sealing carefully to edge of shell. Bake 12 to 15 minutes or until golden brown. Cool. Chill before serving. Refrigerate leftovers.

*Use only Grade A clean, uncracked eggs.

Glazed Strawberry Cheese Pie

CHERRY CHEESE PIE

Makes one 9-inch pie

1 (9-inch) graham cracker crumb
  crust
1 (8-ounce) package cream
  cheese, softened
1 (14-ounce) can Eagle® Brand
  Sweetened Condensed Milk
  (NOT evaporated milk)
⅓ cup ReaLemon® Lemon Juice
  from Concentrate
1 teaspoon vanilla extract
  Canned cherry pie filling,
  chilled

In large bowl, beat cheese until fluffy.
Gradually add sweetened condensed
milk; beat until smooth. Stir in
ReaLemon and vanilla. Pour into
prepared crust. Chill 3 hours or until
set. Top with desired amount of pie
filling before serving. Refrigerate
leftovers.

Topping Variations:

Glazed Strawberry: In small saucepan,
combine 3 tablespoons apple jelly and
1 tablespoon ReaLemon. Cook and stir
until jelly melts. Combine ½ teaspoon
cornstarch and 1 tablespoon water; add
to jelly mixture. Cook and stir until
thickened and clear. Cool 10 minutes.
Arrange sliced strawberries over top of
pie; spoon glaze over strawberries.

Ambrosia: In small saucepan, combine
½ cup peach or apricot preserves, ¼
cup flaked coconut, 2 tablespoons
orange-flavored liqueur and 2 teaspoons cornstarch; cook and stir until
thickened. Remove from heat. Chill
thoroughly. Arrange fresh orange
sections (1 or 2 oranges) on top; drizzle
with sauce. (Makes about ½ cup)

Cranberry Nut: In small bowl, combine
1 cup chilled cranberry-orange relish,
½ cup chopped walnuts and 1 teaspoon
grated orange rind. Spread over pie.
Garnish with orange twists if desired.
(Makes about 1 cup)

Ambrosia Cheese Pie

Cherry Cheese Pie

CITRUS CHESS PIE

Makes one 9-inch pie

1 (9-inch) unbaked pastry shell, pricked
½ cup milk
2 slices white bread
1¼ cups sugar
½ cup margarine or butter, softened
4 eggs
⅓ cup orange juice
⅓ cup ReaLemon® Lemon Juice from Concentrate

Preheat oven to 425°. Bake pastry shell 8 minutes; remove from oven. Reduce oven temperature to 350°. Meanwhile, in small bowl, pour milk over bread; set aside. In large mixer bowl, beat sugar and margarine until fluffy. Add eggs, 1 at a time; beat well. Squeeze milk from bread; crumble into small pieces. Add bread, orange juice and ReaLemon to egg mixture; mix well. Pour into prepared pastry shell; bake 40 to 45 minutes or until knife inserted near center comes out clean. Cool. Refrigerate leftovers.

LEMON SPONGE PIE

Makes one 9-inch pie

1 (9-inch) unbaked pastry shell, pricked
1 cup sugar
¼ cup unsifted flour
¼ cup margarine or butter, melted
2 eggs, separated
⅓ cup ReaLemon® Lemon Juice from Concentrate
1 cup milk

Preheat oven to 350°. Bake pastry shell 8 minutes; remove from oven. Meanwhile, in large mixer bowl, combine sugar, flour, margarine and egg yolks; beat well. Stir in ReaLemon. Gradually add milk; mix well. In small mixer bowl, beat egg whites until stiff but not dry; fold into ReaLemon mixture. Pour into prepared pastry shell; bake 40 minutes or until knife inserted near center comes out clean. Cool. Refrigerate leftovers.

MARGARITA PIE

Makes one 9-inch pie

½ cup margarine or butter
1¼ cups finely crushed pretzels
¼ cup sugar
1 (14-ounce) can Eagle® Brand
  Sweetened Condensed Milk
  (NOT evaporated milk)
⅓ cup ReaLime® Lime Juice from
  Concentrate
2 to 4 tablespoons tequila
2 tablespoons triple sec or other
  orange-flavored liqueur
1 cup (½ pint) whipping cream,
  whipped
  Additional whipped cream,
  orange twists and mint
  leaves or pretzels for
  garnish, optional

In small saucepan, melt margarine; stir
in pretzel crumbs and sugar. Mix well.
Press crumbs on bottom and up side of
buttered 9-inch pie plate; chill. In large
bowl, combine sweetened condensed
milk, ReaLime, tequila and triple sec;
mix well. Fold in whipping cream. Pour
into prepared crust. Freeze or chill until
firm, 4 hours in freezer or 2 hours in
refrigerator. Garnish as desired.
Refrigerate or freeze leftovers.

Margarita Pie

LEMON CHIFFON PIE

Makes one 9-inch pie

1 (9-inch) baked pastry shell with
  high crimped edge
1 envelope unflavored gelatine
¾ cup cold water
6 eggs, separated*
1¼ cups sugar
½ cup ReaLemon® Lemon Juice
  from Concentrate
½ teaspoon cream of tartar

In medium saucepan, sprinkle gelatine
over water to soften; let stand 1 minute.
In medium bowl, beat egg yolks, ¾ *cup*
sugar and ReaLemon; set aside. Over
low heat, cook and stir until gelatine
dissolves (mixture will be clear); stir in
egg yolk mixture. Over medium heat,
cook and stir *just* until mixture boils.
Place pan in bowl of ice or refrigerate,
stirring occasionally, until mixture
mounds when dropped from spoon. In
large mixer bowl, beat egg whites with
cream of tartar until soft peaks form.
Gradually add remaining ½ cup sugar,
1 tablespoon at a time, beating until
stiff glossy peaks form. Fold about
one-third egg white mixture into
ReaLemon mixture; fold this mixture
into remaining egg white mixture.
Spoon into prepared pastry shell. Chill
2 hours or until set. Garnish as desired.
Refrigerate leftovers.

*Use only Grade A clean, uncracked
  eggs.

DEEP DISH PEACH PIE ▶

Makes one 8-inch pie

Pastry for 1-crust pie
1 cup plus 1 tablespoon sugar
2 tablespoons cornstarch
6 cups pared, sliced peaches
   (about 3 pounds)
2 tablespoons ReaLemon®
   Lemon Juice from
   Concentrate
2 tablespoons margarine or
   butter, melted
¼ teaspoon almond extract
1 egg yolk plus 2 tablespoons
   water, optional
2 tablespoons sliced almonds

Preheat oven to 375°. In small bowl, combine *1 cup* sugar and cornstarch. In large bowl, toss peaches with ReaLemon; add sugar mixture, margarine and extract. Turn into 8-inch square baking dish. Top with pastry; cut slits near center. Flute edges. Mix egg yolk and water; brush on surface of pie. Sprinkle with remaining *1 tablespoon* sugar and almonds. Bake 45 to 50 minutes or until golden brown.

Canned Peach Pie: Omit fresh peaches. Reserving ½ cup syrup, drain 2 (29-ounce) cans sliced peaches. Combine sugar and cornstarch. Toss peaches with ReaLemon and reserved syrup; stir in sugar mixture, margarine and extract. Proceed as above.

LEMON PASTRY

Makes one 9-inch pastry shell

1 cup unsifted flour
½ teaspoon salt
⅓ cup shortening
1 egg, beaten
1 tablespoon ReaLemon®
   Lemon Juice from
   Concentrate

Preheat oven to 400°. In medium bowl, combine flour and salt; cut in shortening until crumbly. In small bowl, beat egg and ReaLemon. Sprinkle over flour mixture; stir until dough forms a ball. On floured surface, roll out to about ⅛-inch thickness. Line 9-inch pie plate; flute edges. Prick with fork. Bake 12 to 15 minutes or until golden.

FRESH STRAWBERRY PIE ▲

Makes one 9-inch pie

1 (9-inch) baked pastry shell
1 ¼ cups sugar
1 tablespoon cornstarch
1 ½ cups water
3 tablespoons ReaLemon®
    Lemon Juice from
    Concentrate
1 (3-ounce) package strawberry
    flavor gelatin
1 quart fresh strawberries,
    cleaned and hulled

In medium saucepan, combine sugar
and cornstarch; add water and
ReaLemon. Over high heat, bring to a
boil. Reduce heat; cook and stir until
slightly thickened and clear, 4 to 5
minutes. Add gelatin; stir until dissolved. Cool to room temperature. Stir
in strawberries; turn into prepared
pastry shell. Chill 4 to 6 hours or until
set. Serve with whipped cream if
desired. Refrigerate leftovers.

FROZEN LEMON CREAM PIE

Makes one 9-inch pie

1 (9-inch) graham cracker crumb
    crust
3 eggs, separated*
½ cup plus 2 tablespoons sugar
¼ cup ReaLemon® Lemon Juice
    from Concentrate
1 cup (½ pint) whipping cream,
    whipped

In large mixer bowl, beat egg yolks and
½ *cup* sugar until light; stir in
ReaLemon. In small mixer bowl, beat
egg whites until soft peaks form;
gradually add remaining 2 *tablespoons*
sugar, beating until stiff peaks form.
Fold egg white mixture into ReaLemon
mixture; fold in half the whipped cream.
Fold in remaining whipped cream.
Spoon into prepared crust. Freeze 3
hours or until firm. Serve with whipped
cream or Blueberry 'n' Spice Sauce
(page 114).

*Use only Grade A clean, uncracked
  eggs.

APPLE WALNUT UPSIDE-DOWN PIE

Makes one 9-inch pie

Pastry for 2-crust pie
¼ cup firmly packed light brown sugar
2 tablespoons margarine or butter, melted
½ cup chopped walnuts
4 cups pared and sliced all-purpose apples (about 2 pounds)
⅔ to 1 cup granulated sugar
2 to 3 tablespoons flour
2 tablespoons ReaLemon® Lemon Juice from Concentrate
1 teaspoon ground cinnamon

Preheat oven to 400°. In 9-inch pie plate, combine brown sugar and margarine; spread over bottom. Sprinkle nuts evenly over sugar mixture. Divide pastry in half; roll each into 12-inch circle. Carefully line prepared pie plate with 1 pastry circle; *do not press* into nut mixture. Trim even with edge of plate. Combine remaining ingredients; turn into prepared pie plate. Cover with remaining pastry circle; prick with fork. Trim top crust even with edge of plate; seal crust edges with water. Roll edges *toward center* of pie (crust edge should *not* touch rim of plate). Place aluminum foil or baking sheet on bottom oven rack to catch drippings. Bake 40 to 45 minutes or until golden brown. Let stand 2 minutes; carefully run knife tip around plate to loosen pie. Invert onto serving plate. Serve warm with ice cream if desired.

APPLESAUCE SPICE PIE

Makes one 9-inch pie

1 (9-inch) unbaked pastry shell
1 (15-ounce) jar applesauce
¾ cup firmly packed light brown sugar
4 eggs, beaten
¼ cup ReaLemon® Lemon Juice from Concentrate
2 tablespoons margarine or butter, melted
1 tablespoon flour
¾ teaspoon salt
½ teaspoon ground cinnamon
¼ teaspoon ground nutmeg

Preheat oven to 425°. In large mixer bowl, combine all ingredients except pastry shell; mix well. Pour into pastry shell. Bake 15 minutes; reduce oven temperature to 325°. Continue baking 30 minutes or until wooden pick inserted 2 inches from edge comes out clean. Cool. Serve warm with ice cream or whipped cream if desired. Refrigerate leftovers.

Apple Walnut Upside-Down Pie

Desserts

Company-special cheesecakes, quick fruit compotes and family-pleasing ice creams and sherbets offer an array of desserts for any occasion. Try our luscious Lemon Cream with summer's bountiful fresh fruits. Lemon adds the just-right flavor to desserts for any season.

TRADITIONAL CHEESECAKE

Makes one 9-inch cheesecake

¼ cup margarine or butter, melted
1½ cups graham cracker crumbs
1¾ cups sugar
3 (8-ounce) packages cream cheese, softened
4 eggs
¼ cup ReaLemon® Lemon Juice from Concentrate
¾ teaspoon vanilla extract
Peach Melba Topping*

Preheat oven to 300°. In small bowl, combine margarine, crumbs and ¼ *cup* sugar; pat firmly on bottom of 9-inch springform pan. In large mixer bowl, beat cheese until fluffy. Beat in remaining 1½ *cups* sugar and eggs until smooth. On low speed, add ReaLemon and vanilla; mix well. Pour into prepared pan. Bake 1 hour and 5 to 10 minutes or until cake springs back when lightly touched. Carefully loosen top of cheesecake from edge of pan with knife tip. Cool to room temperature; chill. Serve with Peach Melba Topping. Refrigerate leftovers.

*Peach Melba Topping: Reserve ⅔ cup syrup drained from 1 (10-ounce) package thawed frozen red raspberries. In small saucepan, combine reserved syrup, ¼ cup currant jelly and 1 tablespoon cornstarch. Cook and stir until slightly thick and clear. Cool. Stir in raspberries. Drain 1 (16-ounce) can peach slices; top cake with peach slices and sauce.

Pictured: Traditional Cheesecake, Creamy Lemon and Lime Sherbets (recipe page 110).

CREAMY LEMON SHERBET

Makes about 3 cups

1 cup sugar
2 cups (1 pint) whipping cream,
unwhipped
½ cup ReaLemon® Lemon Juice
from Concentrate
Few drops yellow food coloring

In medium bowl, combine sugar and cream, stirring until dissolved. Stir in ReaLemon and food coloring. Pour into 8-inch square pan or directly into sherbet dishes. Freeze 3 hours or until firm. Remove from freezer 5 minutes before serving. Return leftovers to freezer.

Lime Sherbet: Substitute ReaLime® Lime Juice from Concentrate for ReaLemon and green food coloring for yellow.

APPLE CRISP

Makes 4 to 6 servings

½ to ¾ cup granulated sugar
1 tablespoon cornstarch
¾ teaspoon ground cinnamon
⅓ cup ReaLemon® Lemon Juice
from Concentrate
6 cups pared and sliced all-
purpose apples (about 2½
pounds)
⅓ cup raisins
1 cup quick-cooking oats
½ cup unsifted flour
⅓ cup firmly packed light
brown sugar
¼ teaspoon ground nutmeg
⅓ cup margarine or butter,
melted

Preheat oven to 350°. In small saucepan, combine granulated sugar, cornstarch and *½ teaspoon* cinnamon. Gradually add ReaLemon; mix well. Over medium heat, bring to a boil; cook and stir until slightly thickened and clear. In large bowl, combine apples, raisins and ReaLemon mixture; mix well. Turn into 8-inch square baking dish. In small bowl, combine remaining ingredients; sprinkle evenly over apples. Bake 30 to 40 minutes or until apples are tender. Serve warm with cream or ice cream if desired.

Peach Crisp: Omit raisins. Substitute *6 cups* sliced fresh peaches (about 2½ pounds) for apples. Proceed as above.

MICROWAVE: In medium bowl, combine ReaLemon, cornstarch, sugar and ½ teaspoon cinnamon; mix well. Microwave on full power (high) 2 minutes, stirring after 1 minute. Stir in apples and raisins; turn into 8-inch baking dish; top with oat mixture (directions above). Microwave on full power (high) 14 to 15 minutes or until bubbly.

Apple Crisp

CHAMPAGNE ICE ▲

Makes 6 to 8 servings

**1 (350 mL) bottle champagne
(about 1 ½ cups)**
1 cup water
¾ cup sugar
**¼ cup ReaLime® Lime Juice
from Concentrate**
2 egg whites*
2 tablespoons sugar
**Kiwi fruit and orange slices for
garnish, optional**

In medium bowl, combine champagne,
water, sugar and ReaLime; stir until
sugar dissolves. In small mixer bowl,
beat egg whites until soft peaks form;
gradually add sugar, beating until stiff
but not dry. Fold into champagne
mixture (egg whites float to surface).
Pour into individual serving dishes.
Freeze. Remove from freezer 5 to 10
minutes before serving. Garnish as
desired.

Tip: Mixture can be poured into 2-quart
shallow baking dish; cover and freeze.
Remove from freezer 15 to 20 minutes
before serving; cut into squares. Return
leftovers to freezer.

*Use only Grade A clean, uncracked
eggs.

STRAWBERRY ICE ▲

Makes 6 servings

**1 quart strawberries, cleaned
and hulled**
1 cup sugar
½ cup water
**3 tablespoons ReaLemon®
Lemon Juice from
Concentrate**
**Few drops red food coloring,
optional**

In blender container, combine sugar,
water and ReaLemon; mix well. Gradually add strawberries; blend until
smooth, adding food coloring if
desired. Pour into 8-inch square pan;
freeze about 1 ½ hours. In small mixer
bowl, beat until slushy. Return to
freezer. Place in refrigerator 1 hour
before serving to soften. Return
leftovers to freezer.

LUSCIOUS LEMON CREAM ▲

Makes about 3 cups

2 eggs
1 cup sugar
⅓ cup ReaLemon® Lemon Juice
   from Concentrate
1 tablespoon cornstarch
½ cup water
1 teaspoon vanilla extract
1 cup (½ pint) whipping cream,
   whipped

In small bowl, beat eggs, ½ cup sugar
and ReaLemon until foamy; set aside.
In medium saucepan, combine remaining ½ cup sugar and cornstarch.
Gradually add water; mix well. Over
medium heat, cook and stir until
thickened and clear; remove from heat.
Gradually beat in egg mixture. Over
low heat, cook and stir until slightly
thickened. Remove from heat; stir in
vanilla. Cool. Fold whipped cream into
sauce. Chill. Serve with fresh fruit.
Refrigerate leftovers.

HOT FRUIT COMPOTE

Makes 8 to 10 servings

1 (20-ounce) can pineapple
   chunks, drained
1 (17-ounce) can pitted dark
   sweet cherries, drained
1 (16-ounce) can sliced peaches,
   drained
1 (16-ounce) can pear halves,
   drained
1 (11-ounce) can mandarin
   orange segments, drained
¼ cup margarine or butter
½ cup firmly packed light brown
   sugar
½ cup orange juice
¼ cup ReaLemon® Lemon Juice
   from Concentrate
½ teaspoon ground cinnamon
   Sour cream and brown sugar

Preheat oven to 350°. In 13x9-inch
baking dish, combine fruits. In small
saucepan, melt margarine; add sugar,
orange juice, ReaLemon and cinnamon.
Pour mixture over fruits. Bake 20
minutes or until hot. Serve warm with
sour cream and brown sugar.

BREAD PUDDING WITH LEMON RAISIN SAUCE

Makes 6 servings

4 cups whole wheat bread cubes (about 8 slices)
4 eggs, slightly beaten
2¾ cups milk
½ cup firmly packed light brown sugar
1½ teaspoons ground cinnamon
2 tablespoons ReaLemon® Lemon Juice from Concentrate
Lemon Raisin Sauce

Preheat oven to 350°. Arrange bread cubes in lightly greased 9-inch square baking pan. In medium bowl, combine eggs, milk, sugar and cinnamon; mix well. Add ReaLemon; mix well. Pour over bread cubes. Bake 45 minutes or until knife inserted near center comes out clean. Serve warm with whipped cream or topping and Lemon Raisin Sauce. Refrigerate leftovers.

Lemon Raisin Sauce

½ cup granulated sugar
¼ cup firmly packed light brown sugar
2 tablespoons cornstarch
¾ cup water
¼ cup ReaLemon® Lemon Juice from Concentrate
¼ cup raisins
2 tablespoons margarine or butter

In small saucepan, combine sugars and cornstarch. Gradually add water and ReaLemon; mix well. Over medium heat, cook and stir until mixture comes to a boil. Reduce heat; continue cooking and stirring 3 to 4 minutes or until thick and clear. Stir in raisins and margarine. Serve warm over bread pudding. (Makes about 1½ cups)

SPICED LEMON PEARS

Makes 4 servings

1½ cups water
1 cup firmly packed light brown sugar
¼ cup ReaLemon® Lemon Juice from Concentrate
2 cinnamon sticks
6 whole cloves
4 fresh pears, halved, pared and core removed

In large saucepan, combine all ingredients except pears. Bring to a boil; cook and stir until sugar dissolves. Add pears; cover and simmer 10 minutes or until pears are tender. Serve warm or chilled as a dessert, meat accompaniment or salad.

MICROWAVE: In 2-quart round baking dish, combine all ingredients except pears. Cover with plastic wrap; microwave on full power (high) 6 minutes or until mixture boils. Stir; add pears. Cover; microwave 6 minutes or until tender. Proceed as above.

Bread Pudding with Lemon Raisin Sauce

Lemon Ice Cream with Blueberry 'n' Spice Sauce

LEMON ANGEL CREAM CAKE

Makes one 13x9-inch cake

1 envelope unflavored gelatine
¼ cup cold water
6 eggs, separated
1 cup sugar
½ cup ReaLemon® Lemon Juice from Concentrate
1 (14-ounce) prepared angel food cake, cut in 1-inch pieces
1 (10-ounce) package frozen strawberries or red raspberries in syrup, thawed

Soften gelatine in water. In medium saucepan, beat egg yolks and ¼ cup sugar until foamy. Add ReaLemon; mix well. Over low heat, cook and stir until slightly thickened, about 10 minutes; remove from heat. Add gelatine; stir until dissolved. Cool. In large mixer bowl, beat egg whites until foamy. Gradually add remaining ¾ cup sugar, beating until stiff but not dry. Fold ReaLemon mixture into egg whites. Fold in cake pieces. Spoon into 13x9-inch baking dish. Chill 4 hours or until set. Cut into squares. Serve with strawberries. Refrigerate leftovers.

LEMON ICE CREAM

Makes about 1½ quarts

3 egg yolks*
1 (14-ounce) can Eagle® Brand Sweetened Condensed Milk (NOT evaporated milk)
½ cup ReaLemon® Lemon Juice from Concentrate
Few drops yellow food coloring, optional
2 cups (1 pint) whipping cream, whipped

In large bowl, beat egg yolks; stir in sweetened condensed milk, ReaLemon and food coloring. Fold in whipped cream. Pour into 9x5-inch loaf pan or other 2-quart container. Cover; freeze 6 hours or until firm. Serve with warm Blueberry 'n' Spice Sauce.

*Use only Grade A clean, uncracked eggs.

BLUEBERRY 'N' SPICE SAUCE

Makes about 1⅔ cups

½ cup sugar
1 tablespoon cornstarch
½ teaspoon ground cinnamon
¼ teaspoon ground nutmeg
¼ cup hot water
2 tablespoons ReaLemon® Lemon Juice from Concentrate
2 cups fresh or dry-pack frozen blueberries, rinsed and drained

In small saucepan, combine sugar, cornstarch, cinnamon and nutmeg; gradually stir in water and ReaLemon. Over medium heat, cook, stirring constantly, until mixture thickens and comes to a boil. Add blueberries; cook and stir until mixture comes to a boil. Serve warm over ice cream or cake.

MICROWAVE: In 1-quart glass measure, combine sugar, cornstarch, cinnamon and nutmeg. Gradually add water and ReaLemon. Microwave on full power (high) 2 to 3 minutes or until mixture boils. Stir in blueberries; microwave on full power (high) 2 minutes or until mixture boils. Proceed as above.

FROZEN LEMON SOUFFLE

Makes 6 to 8 servings

1½ cups sugar
3 tablespoons cornstarch
1 envelope unflavored gelatine
1 cup water
⅔ cup ReaLemon® Lemon Juice
   from Concentrate *or*
   ReaLime® Lime Juice from
   Concentrate
Few drops yellow or green food
   coloring, optional
3 egg whites*
1 cup (½ pint) whipping cream

In large saucepan, combine sugar, cornstarch and gelatine; add water and ReaLemon. Over medium heat, cook and stir until slightly thickened; stir in food coloring. Cool. Chill until partially set, about 1 hour, stirring occasionally. In small mixer bowl, beat egg whites until stiff but not dry; fold into ReaLemon mixture. In small mixer bowl, beat whipping cream until stiff peaks form; fold into ReaLemon mixture. Tape or tie a 3-inch wax paper or aluminum foil "collar" securely around rim of 1-quart souffle dish. Pour mixture into dish. Freeze 6 hours or overnight. Remove "collar." Garnish with whipped cream, candy lemon drops and gum drop slivers if desired. Return leftovers to freezer.

Tip: Souffle can be chilled in refrigerator 6 hours instead of frozen.

*Use only Grade A clean, uncracked eggs.

CREAMY BAKED CHEESECAKE

Makes one 9-inch cheesecake

- ⅓ cup margarine or butter, melted
- 1¼ cups graham cracker crumbs
- ¼ cup sugar
- 2 (8-ounce) packages cream cheese, softened
- 1 (14-ounce) can Eagle® Brand Sweetened Condensed Milk (NOT evaporated milk)
- 3 eggs
- ¼ cup ReaLemon® Lemon Juice from Concentrate
- 1 (8-ounce) container sour cream

Continued next column

Creamy Baked Cheesecake

Preheat oven to 300°. Combine margarine, crumbs and sugar; pat firmly on bottom of 9-inch springform pan. In large mixer bowl, beat cheese until fluffy. Gradually add sweetened condensed milk; beat until smooth. Add eggs and ReaLemon; mix well. Pour into prepared pan. Bake 50 to 55 minutes or until cake springs back when lightly touched. Turn oven off. To minimize cracking, leave cheesecake in oven 1 hour. Cool to room temperature. Chill. Remove side of pan. Spread sour cream on cheesecake. Garnish as desired. Refrigerate leftovers.

New York Style Cheesecake: Omit sour cream. Preheat oven to 350°. Beat 4 (8-ounce) packages cream cheese until fluffy. Beat in 2 tablespoons flour then 4 eggs. Gradually add sweetened condensed milk; beat until smooth. Add ¼ cup ReaLemon; mix well. Pour into prepared pan. Bake 60 minutes or until light golden brown. Cool to room temperature. Chill. Garnish as desired.

RICH LEMON PUDDING SAUCE

Makes about 3½ cups

- **2 cups sugar**
- **¾ cup margarine or butter**
- **⅔ cup ReaLemon® Lemon Juice from Concentrate**
- **6 eggs**

In medium saucepan, combine sugar, margarine and ReaLemon. Over low heat, cook, stirring constantly, until sugar dissolves and margarine melts. In small bowl, beat eggs until light and lemon-colored. Gradually stir about *¼ cup* hot mixture into eggs; stir into remaining ReaLemon mixture. Over medium heat, cook, stirring constantly, until thick and creamy, about 5 to 12 minutes. Chill. Serve warm or chilled over cake or ice cream. Refrigerate leftovers.

Tip: Chilled sauce can be used as a pudding, to fill tart shells or cake layers.

Continued next column

Rich Lemon Pudding Sauce

MICROWAVE: In 2-quart round baking dish, cover margarine with wax paper; microwave on full power (high) 1 minute or until melted. Stir in ReaLemon and sugar; microwave 2½ minutes on full power (high) or until sugar dissolves. In small bowl, beat eggs until light and lemon-colored. Gradually stir about ¼ cup hot mixture into eggs; stir into remaining ReaLemon mixture. Microwave on ⅔ power (medium-high) 5 to 7 minutes or until thick, stirring every minute. Proceed as above.

Etc...

Refreshing Salad Dressing

Use ReaLemon for a light-tasting alternative to vinegar when preparing your favorite homemade salad dressing or packaged mix. Just substitute an equal amount of ReaLemon for vinegar.

Mushroom Lovers

In medium saucepan, bring ⅓ cup water, 2 tablespoons ReaLemon, 1 tablespoon butter and a dash salt to a boil. Add whole or sliced fresh mushrooms. Cover and simmer 5 minutes; stir occasionally. Serve as a garnish or side dish.

Refreshing Water

Add ReaLemon to hot or cold water for a refreshing low calorie beverage.

Tea & Lemon

Add a few drops ReaLemon to iced or hot tea to enhance the flavor. Or freeze ReaLemon in ice cube trays to use in iced tea.

Buttermilk Substitution

When a recipe calls for buttermilk or sour milk, combine 1 tablespoon ReaLemon plus milk to make 1 cup. Let stand 5 minutes and mixture will be thick and ready to use.

Low Sodium Tip

Cutting down on sodium? Try sprinkling ReaLemon instead of salt on vegetables to enhance the flavor.

Reduce Onion Odors

To reduce onion and garlic odors, rinse hands and cutting board with ReaLemon and cold water when peeling, slicing or grating onions or garlic.

Reduce Fish Odors

To eliminate fishy odor and taste, brush fish with ReaLemon before cooking, or add ReaLemon to cold oil or butter before frying.

Diet Soda Perk-up

Add lemony freshness to diet sodas, club soda or other carbonated beverages by adding a few drops ReaLemon or ReaLime.

Apples For Pie

To give ordinary eating apples the tartness of "pie apples," sprinkle 1 tablespoon ReaLemon over sliced apples.

Barbecue Tip

When barbecuing or broiling chicken or other poultry, brush with ReaLemon for added flavor and moistness.

Warm Punch

To help keep warm punch warm, and to "condition" a glass bowl for a hot punch, slowly pour very warm water into punch bowl and let stand until bowl is warmed.

Savory Lemon Ice Cubes

To make ice cubes for unsweetened drinks, like Bloody Marys, combine 1 part water, and 1 part ReaLemon in ice cube trays; place olive, pearl onion or celery in each section if desired. Freeze.

Keep Fruits Bright

To keep fruit garnishes such as apple slices or wedges, banana slices, etc. from darkening, dip in ReaLemon.

Punch Ice Ring

To make a fruited ice ring for punches, add ReaLemon to ring mold to ½ inch.

Arrange fruits and mint leaves in mold. Freeze.

Add water to fill mold. Freeze until solid.

To unmold ice ring, quickly dip in hot water. Turn into punch bowl.

Iced Tea Cubes

In 1-quart pitcher, combine 3 cups strong brewed tea, cooled, and ¼ cup ReaLemon. Pour into ice cube trays. Place 1 piece of fruit (maraschino cherries, mandarin orange segments, etc.) in each section if desired. Freeze. Use in iced tea. Makes about 3 dozen.

Lemon Ice Cubes

Dissolve ¾ cup sugar in 1 cup ReaLemon; add 3 cups water. Pour into ice cube trays. Place 1 piece fruit in each section. Freeze.

Etc. . .

PEACH FREEZER JAM

Makes about 4 cups

2 cups pared, crushed fresh peaches (about 2 pounds)
3¼ cups sugar
1 (3-fluid ounce) pouch liquid fruit pectin (about 7 tablespoons)
3 tablespoons ReaLemon® Lemon Juice from Concentrate

In large bowl, combine peaches and sugar; mix well. Let stand 10 minutes. In small bowl, combine pectin and ReaLemon; pour over peaches. Stir thoroughly 3 minutes (a few sugar crystals will remain). Spoon into glass or plastic containers; cover. Let stand at room temperature 24 hours. Store in freezer.

Tip: Small amounts can be refrigerated, covered, 2 to 3 weeks.

STRAWBERRY FREEZER JAM

Makes about 4½ cups

2 cups crushed fresh strawberries (about 1½ quarts)
4 cups sugar
1 (3-fluid ounce) pouch liquid fruit pectin (about 7 tablespoons)
2 tablespoons ReaLemon® Lemon Juice from Concentrate

In large bowl, combine strawberries and sugar; mix well. Let stand 10 minutes. In small bowl, combine pectin and ReaLemon; pour over strawberries. Stir thoroughly 3 minutes (a few sugar crystals will remain). Spoon into glass or plastic containers; cover. Let stand at room temperature 24 hours. Store in freezer.

Tip: Small amounts can be refrigerated, covered, 2 to 3 weeks.

LEMON MARSHMALLOW SAUCE

Makes about 1 cup

1 (7-ounce) jar marshmallow creme
3 tablespoons ReaLemon® Lemon Juice from Concentrate

In small bowl, combine ingredients; mix well. Chill to blend flavors. Serve over fruit, ice cream or cake.

LEMON WHIPPED CREAM

Makes about 2 cups

1 cup (½ pint) whipping cream
1 tablespoon ReaLemon® Lemon Juice from Concentrate
2 tablespoons sugar

In small mixer bowl, combine cream and ReaLemon; beat until soft peaks form. Gradually add sugar, beating *only* until stiff. Serve with fruit, baked or steamed puddings, pies or cakes. Refrigerate leftovers.

REALEMON STARTS WITH FRESH LEMONS

ReaLemon starts with the juice of fresh lemons, concentrated to a uniform strength. Enough filtered water is used to return this concentrate to the natural strength of fresh lemons. Lemon oil from the peel is added to enhance the natural taste of fresh lemons.

ReaLemon is more economical and more convenient than home-squeezed lemons. And since fresh lemons can differ in size, juiciness, and strength, the uniformity of ReaLemon can be an advantage in preparing recipes that call for lemon juice. For recipes specifying the "juice of one lemon," use 2 to 3 tablespoons of ReaLemon.

HORSERADISH LEMON CREAM

Makes about 2 cups

**1 cup (½ pint) whipping cream
1 tablespoon ReaLemon® Lemon
Juice from Concentrate
2 teaspoons prepared horseradish, drained**

In small mixer bowl, combine cream
and ReaLemon; beat *only* until stiff.
Fold in horseradish. Serve with roast
beef, corned beef, ham or ham loaf.
Refrigerate leftovers.

Lemon Rice

For a refreshing flavor change, combine
1 cup long grain rice with ¾ cup water,
¼ cup ReaLemon and 1 Wyler's®
Chicken-Flavor Bouillon Cube. Bring to
a boil; cover and simmer 15 to 20
minutes or until liquid is absorbed. Stir
in chopped water chestnuts, pimiento
and parsley if desired.

Surprise Glazed Chicken

Spread a mixture of ReaLemon, mayonnaise and Parmesan cheese on a roasted
chicken. Return to oven; bake 10
minutes longer.

Quick Saucy Vegetables

For vegetables with a new flavor twist,
mix ReaLemon and chopped onion with
sour cream—stir into cooked green
beans, lima beans or broccoli.

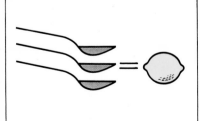

About 3 tablespoons of ReaLemon®
Lemon Juice from Concentrate
equals the juice of one lemon.

On A Diet?

Use ReaLemon on your salads instead
of high calorie salad dressing. And try
ReaLemon on seafood in place of tartar
sauce.

Lemon & Melon

Squeeze a few drops of ReaLemon or
ReaLime onto cantaloupe, honeydew
or other melon to complement the fruit
flavor.

Index

REALEMON 50TH ANNIVERSARY RECIPE COLLECTION

BUY: 2—50th Anniversary Bottles, any size, ReaLemon® Lemon Juice from
   Concentrate **or** ReaLime® Lime Juice from Concentrate

SEND: $2.95 + 2—50th Anniversary labels **or** $4.95 with no proofs
   of purchase

RECEIVE: Realemon 50th Anniversary Recipe Collection

MAIL TO: ReaLemon Recipe Collection
   P.O. Box 8990-D
   Clinton, IA 52736   Name: _____

Allow 6 weeks for delivery.   Address: _____
Offer good only in U.S.A while
supplies last. Void where
restricted.   City: _____ State _____ Zip _____

REALEMON 50TH ANNIVERSARY RECIPE COLLECTION

BUY: 2—50th Anniversary Bottles, any size, ReaLemon® Lemon Juice from
   Concentrate **or** ReaLime® Lime Juice from Concentrate

SEND: $2.95 + 2—50th Anniversary labels **or** $4.95 with no proofs
   of purchase

RECEIVE: Realemon 50th Anniversary Recipe Collection

MAIL TO: ReaLemon Recipe Collection
   P.O. Box 8990-D
   Clinton, IA 52736   Name: _____

Allow 6 weeks for delivery.   Address: _____
Offer good only in U.S.A while
supplies last. Void where
restricted.   City: _____ State _____ Zip _____

REALEMON 50TH ANNIVERSARY RECIPE COLLECTION

BUY: 2—50th Anniversary Bottles, any size, ReaLemon® Lemon Juice from
   Concentrate **or** ReaLime® Lime Juice from Concentrate

SEND: $2.95 + 2—50th Anniversary labels **or** $4.95 with no proofs
   of purchase

RECEIVE: Realemon 50th Anniversary Recipe Collection

MAIL TO: ReaLemon Recipe Collection
   P.O. Box 8990-D
   Clinton, IA 52736   Name: _____

Allow 6 weeks for delivery.   Address: _____
Offer good only in U.S.A while
supplies last. Void where
restricted.   City: _____ State _____ Zip _____

REALEMON 50TH ANNIVERSARY RECIPE COLLECTION

BUY: 2—50th Anniversary Bottles, any size, ReaLemon® Lemon Juice from
   Concentrate **or** ReaLime® Lime Juice from Concentrate

SEND: $2.95 + 2—50th Anniversary labels **or** $4.95 with no proofs
   of purchase

RECEIVE: Realemon 50th Anniversary Recipe Collection

MAIL TO: ReaLemon Recipe Collection
   P.O. Box 8990-D
   Clinton, IA 52736   Name: _____

Allow 6 weeks for delivery.   Address: _____
Offer good only in U.S.A while
supplies last. Void where
restricted.   City: _____ State _____ Zip _____

Order Forms for the REALEMON Recipe Collection.